Prayer, Politics, and Power

PRAYER, POLITICS & POWER

Joel C. Hunter

Tyndale House Publishers, Inc.
Wheaton, Illinois

Unless otherwise noted, Scripture quotations in this book are taken from the *New American Standard Bible,* copyright 1960, 1962, 1963, 1968, 1971, 1972, 1973 by The Lockman Foundation. Quotations marked KJV are from the King James Version of the Bible.

First printing, February 1988

Library of Congress Catalog Card Number 87-51592
ISBN 0-8423-4973-1

Printed in the United States of America

Contents

PART II
After Analysis, Action

Preface

Something was different about Dr. Stanley J. Shoemaker as he stood behind his high pulpit that Sunday. I looked around First Methodist Church, Shelby, Ohio, as I did every Sunday as a boy. Everyone looked so perfect. The men were in suits formal enough for a funeral. White collars were more than their categories of work. Those collars were symbols of self-confidence and sophistication.

The ladies lifted their stately heads to the Reverend Doctor in the pulpit. The fruit on their hats tilted ever so slightly upwards. I looked to Dr. Shoemaker, too, for another distinguished but indistinguishable message. His robed arms braced him as he leaned toward us. The tone of his voice braced us all as he spoke the opening words. Then Dr. Shoemaker let go of a sermon the likes of which I had never heard. Gone were the usual long, academic words like *redemptive intent* and *eschatological hope* and *alienation*. Here came words like *sin* and *repent* and *you*.

Men folded their arms across their chests. Women let their mouths drift open in disbelief. The emotional temperature was rising to the point that the fruit on their hats could have gone the way of cherries jubilee. And then, the ultimate surprise—Dr. Shoemaker gave an altar call. He asked for any to come forward and confess faith in Christ. The tension was so thick you could have knelt on it. A voice inside me urged me to go. I looked around once more, hoping that someone would lead the way. As the hymn verses pushed on, it was apparent that no one was going to visibly respond. My insides wrestled for a decision, but neither side won during the closing verses and benediction.

Dr. Shoemaker went away discouraged. To my knowledge, he never tried that again at First Church. That Sunday's invitation, however, never left me. It created a hunger within me for the deep and significant matters of life.

Years later I was a freshman at Ohio University. It was the mid-1960s. The United States was making new policies left and right, mostly right. The students were polarized left and right, mostly left. Armed forces had just entered into Cambodia. Students entered into intense political analysis. The student leaders I heard were most eloquent and serious. They spoke of deep and significant issues: of how people ought to be, of how government was so wrong, of what better ideas young people have. Though I was against the extremist factions of the movement, I was drawn into the center that reasoned for solutions and was impassioned for results. I had found my cause. I placed all my hope in political philosophies led by new and improved personalities—like Robert Kennedy and Martin Luther King, Jr.

But a strange thing happened on the way to Utopia. In all of the wonderfully intense idealism, we missed something that could ruin everything. What was it that made my heroes get killed? What was it that turned the reasoned, positive, uplifting dreams into verbal weapons of cynicism and bitterness? The rhetoric had changed from "this is how to improve what we have now" to "this is how to destroy what we have now." The student leaders began to debate and attack one another. What was it that disintegrated altruism into egotism? A major part of the leaders' solutions had turned into personal ambition. All was being corrupted. What was it that was tainting every good effort?

For the first time I came to realize the social and personal devastation of sin. I marveled at its depth and subtlety. I had heard enough descriptions of it to remember its characteristics. I had remembered enough of Dr. Shoemaker's invitation to know the solution.

One night I walked the aisle to a generic altar in the university's Galbreath Chapel. There I responded to Dr. Shoemaker's altar call of years before. Alone in the chapel, I knelt and placed all my confidence in Christ.

I did not abandon hope of an improved political structure. I majored in history and government, though after my experience in the chapel I put them into a new perspective. I knew that improvements in our government for any major change in people were too simplistic and unrealistic.

The prelude to this work then is both theoretical and personal. My journey was from political idealism, through disillusionment, to the Lord of the universe who is stationed in the heart. I see some evangelical Christians tempted to reverse that order of progress in the name of "practical Christianity." It is especially for those that this volume is written.

Introduction

We in the United States are entering a new era in our government's development. The political forces in the last decade of this century will be unlike those that have come before, especially in the area of religion and politics. We will be facing emotional issues that could overwhelm us. We can anticipate sharply divisive times if we do not define now a common understanding of both of these realms of authority. The potential problem does not lie, as many believe, in mixing religion and politics. The problem comes in mixing them up, in confusing one with the other.

This work attempts to clarify the important interplay of religion and politics in our society. When we talk of religion, we will be talking about Christianity. Yet many of the same principles and cautions could apply to other faiths if God chose to let them be determinative in our country's future. When we talk of politics we will be confining most remarks to the electoral process. While the judicial branch of our government is ultimately responsible for defining the meaning of "separation of church and state," the scope of this work is confined to issues concerning elected officials. It must be remembered, though, that election results affect future court decisions.

It is also important to note that both the style and content of this volume are intended to serve the thinking believer. It is not intended mainly for the academician, though its theories will interest one. Rather, it is intended for the voter especially interested in understanding these issues and acting on that understanding. As you will read, there is at least as much reason to be active as there is to be careful.

PART I

Politics and Piety under the Lens

If you read history you will find that the Christians who did most for the present world were precisely those who thought most of the next. It is since Christians have largely ceased to think of the other world that they have become so ineffective in this.

C. S. LEWIS

Commitment to Christ must involve commitment to our neighbor and our world, for Christ's sake.

LEIGHTON FORD

ONE

Right Wing—Wrong Bird

Judge eternal, throned in splendor,
Lord of lords and King of kings,
With your living fire of judgment
Purge this land of bitter things;
Solace all its wide dominion
With the healing of your wings.

Henry S. *Holland* (1847–1918)

Many of us are apprehensive about the future. Some grave problems afflict our society, and we know it is our responsibility to address them. We could escape our responsibility by handing them to God with some neat Christian cliche like, "I don't know what the future holds, but I know Who holds the future." We have a distinct sense, however, that God calls for our involvement as well as our confidence. We would be glad to take corrective measures if we knew what measures would be most effective.

Many Christians are becoming involved. Led by the evangelicals, they form a religiopolitical team that is growing into a significant force. They are a new, fervent, focused power in the American political process. There are even religious leaders of celebrity status in positions that would enable them to run for the top offices of the land. There are specific groups of

Christians with specific political strategies, trying for specific political offices and for specifically religious reasons. That kind of direct, practical action should make Christians feel that we have representation in government and an expressway to involvement when we choose to get active.

But some of us are still apprehensive. It is not that we think these involved evangelicals are wrong. We agree with so much of what they have to say. Yet hopping on the bandwagon does not feel quite right either. We need to do some thinking first.

The present American political situation is like the treasure containing things both new and old (Matt. 13:52). The current movement by the religious right for political dominion (not just single-issue victories) is new. This country has seen the day of religious magistrates for colonies and intense religious activism toward certain issues throughout its history. But the formulation of a national Christian movement of such sweeping intent is new. The religious mass media give this movement potential for mobilization never before available. Some of us are glad for the accelerating power of this bandwagon. Yet it is new and still unfamiliar, so we wonder, "Does it have any brakes? Does it have a preset course that will take all of us who jump on to conclusions we may not have chosen? Who is driving? Are there better ways than a bandwagon to exert political influence?"

There are old, valuable lessons in the treasure, too. There is wisdom that predates action. This movement in our rather young country is new, but combinations of politics and religion are as old as history. Might we gain some insights that would help us avoid major mistakes in our political enthusiasm? Would not an overview help us spot flaws that could hinder the purposes of both our government and our faith?

Some of us are excited that Christians are not hiding in churches anymore. We are hopeful about Americans being reminded about Christian values while voting. We can see individual Christians being politically competent in the future, having a solid plan instead of a scared reaction. We can even see Christians influencing the manners of politics as well as the policies. Who better could teach others how to understand and love the opposition, if we could just learn it ourselves? First, though, we must think.

We need not analyze every detail, but we do need a closer look at what is integral in the present mix of evangelical Christianity and American politics. There have been several recent and tenuous alliances. Many evangelicals, charismatics, and fundamentalists have allied to form the religious right. The religious right has become allied with the political right to form the right-wing (more conservative or, as some would say, reactionary) political force. In a vague and intuitive way, American people have connected society's failures with Christianity's answers while failing to differentiate between politics and personal faith. More subtly, the Christians have theologically unified and confused the biblical forms of government with America's forms. Keeping these facts in mind, let's begin with a look at just who the evangelicals are.

Who Are the Evangelicals?

When the Gallup organization interviewed Americans in 1984, it defined evangelicals as persons with three basic characteristics. They describe themselves as born-again Christians or say they have had a born-again experience. They encourage other people to believe in Jesus Christ. They believe in a literal interpretation of the Bible.[1] (That last characteristic causes problems, because many evangelicals would not use the term *literal* in interpretation even though they believe the Bible to be the absolute authority of life and the divinely inspired, inerrant Word of God.) The results in 1984 were that 22 percent of Americans, or about 35 million people, described themselves with all three of these characteristics. More specifically, 40 percent said they were born again, 48 percent said they had encouraged others to believe in Christ, and 37 percent said they believed in a literal interpretation of the Bible. That is a significant number of people.

Going beyond that basic definition, evangelical Christians believe that God came to us in Christ (John 1:1, 14). They believe that it was necessary for Him to do so because people's sins separate them from God in such a way that people can never return to Him on their own—neither by good works nor by our self-made religions (Isa. 53:6; 59:2). Evangelicals believe that Christ on the cross made it possible for us to reach God and for Him to reach us—through our unity with Christ whose death has taken away our sins (Rom. 5:8). They believe we are saved (from permanent separation) by God's grace (unmerited favor) through faith in Christ (Eph. 2:8). Evangelicals believe we can be sure of our salvation (1 John 5:11-13) and that our lives are transformed by it (2 Cor. 5:17). They believe that by saying a simple prayer like, "Dear Father, I admit I am a sinner. I believe Jesus Christ died for me. I trust Christ now for the forgiveness of my sins. Come into my life and make of it what you will," and meaning it, anyone is saved. Evangelicals believe the purpose of Christ and His church is to "make disciples of all nations" (Matt. 28:19). A disciple is a learner and follower of Jesus Christ. To that end, they cannot resist offering to share the way to salvation. When one develops as a disciple, one generates all other specific characteristics that give God glory—for example, spiritual maturity, charitable help of neighbors, involvement in community responsibilities, etc. But each of the specifics is done ultimately to glorify God and to bring others to Him.

Also, evangelicals believe in the Bible as God's authoritative revelation. Two points are important here for later discussion. First, evangelicals believe in knowledge that is "revealed" in addition to knowledge that is "natural." Second, evangelicals believe in the Bible as the rule for all of life. It is authoritative. Its truths are the most profound and certain in the world. When the late Karl Barth, one of the world's most brilliant theologians, visited an American seminary years ago, he was asked, "Dr. Barth, what is the most profound religious truth you have experienced in your lifetime?" He paused and thought for several minutes. Then he answered seriously with the lines of a child's song: "Jesus loves me, this I know, for the Bible tells me so."

While we are defining evangelicalism, we need to consider the problem of terminology. Does the name *evangelical* have the same meaning as *fundamentalist* or *charismatic*? This can be confusing, and I offer the following information with the hope that I offend no Christian brother. To begin, evangelicals are not necessarily fundamentalists, though many fundamentalists consider themselves evangelicals. The distinction between evangelicals and fundamentalists is not clear, and secular authors sometimes use the terms interchangeably. Generally, fundamentalists tend to be more conservative about matters of personal morality and less inclined to cater to social and intellectual respectability. Charismatics are those Christians who believe in the baptism of the Spirit, speaking in tongues, and other spiritual gifts that in many churches are not emphasized. While most charismatics would consider themselves evangelicals, many evangelicals would not consider themselves charismatics. Labels are a problem, since they tend to divide us from people that we might have much in common with. (It is possible to be an evangelical *and* fundamentalist *and* charismatic at the same time.) But generally speaking, evangelicals could be seen in a more centrist position in conservative Christianity. The union of politically active evangelicals, fundamentalists, and charismatics will be interesting to watch in the years ahead, especially since they (in spite of differences) emphasize many of the same items on the political agenda. The unity so far has been seen by some as nothing less than a miracle of God.

The Religious Right Plus the Political Right

According to Washington correspondent William Bole, the alliance between the religious and political right-wings began some years ago when political "operatives" in Washington contacted leaders in conservative religious groups. "These efforts led directly to the currently most visible New Christian Right groups: the Moral Majority, Christian Voice, and the Religious Roundtable. . . . Those involved in these organizations found new friends in such secular New Right leaders as

Paul Weyerich, who masterminded the initial marriage between the secular and the religious right, direct-mail whiz Richard Viguerie and Howard Phillips of the Conservative Caucus."[2]

The alliance was immediately effective in aiding in the defeat of several key democrats (George McGovern and others), and in 1984 the organization was critically important in Reagan's support base.

A well-known list of issues unites the political and religious. Among the concerns are abortion, pornography, prayer in public schools, ending state regulation of religious schools, increasing defense spending, and decreasing social welfare spending.

These and other issues are pushing the religious right into a historically unusual activism in politics. Organized Christian involvement has run in cycles and has been more pronounced on the liberal side of the church. The issues in the 1800s included prison reform, women's rights, and care for the mentally insane. At the turn of the century the issues centered around people victimized by industrialization, e.g., improved working conditions, the right to strike, housing the homeless. In the 1960s, liberal Christians were instrumental in the civil rights movement and the protest of the Vietnam War.

The conservative side of Christianity has not been politically vocal since the fundamentalists' efforts in prohibition (trying to ban alcohol consumption) and the infamous 1925 Scopes "Monkey Trial" (trying to eliminate teaching the theory of evolution). The embarrassment of those press images sent them back to dealing with matters in the church. Until the late 1970s, conservatives were much less likely to be politically active than their liberal counterparts. In 1968 a survey[3] taken of clergy included the familiar cliche, "If people would just love one another, the social ills would take care of themselves." The results found 44 percent of the clergy agreeing with that statement, but of that percentage, 77 percent were conservative and only 7 percent were liberals. (That kind of platitude participation is reflected in a comment Will Rogers is said to have made in response to the German submarine problem during World War I. He theorized a simple solution: "Simply boil the ocean and when they come to the surface we can shoot them." Someone asked, "How do you boil the ocean?" Rogers responded, "Look, I've given you the solution. It's up to you to work out the details!")

In the years before the 1970s, the religiously conservative electorate was more prone to name solutions than details. But things have changed. Contrast a 1980 ABC-Lou Harris poll in which 74 percent of white evangelicals agreed "it is fitting and proper for religious groups to support candidates and to be politically active to restore morality to public life." In the American tradition of pragmatism, the religious right is bonding with political means to change the nation. What happened?

The Relapse-Religion Connection

The recent succession of Supreme Court decisions that subtract the tradition of religion from our society have frightened concerned evangelicals. Evangelicals are not against abortion simply because they are on the conservative side of issues; they believe it is legalized murder. Evangelicals are not alarmed at the elimination of prayer from school simply because they don't want things to change; they believe religion is the expression of truth. To many we are not just beginning to eliminate optional opinion, we are beginning to undermine the foundational principles upon which our stability as a nation stands.

The evangelicals are not the only ones becoming uneasy with the trends in society. For most Americans, the speed at which things are changing is unnerving. The various "rights" movements and the divorce rate have confronted us all with the hazards of "me and my rights" assertiveness. Is this assertiveness simply a continuation of the rugged individualism so necessary for survival in the early (and isolated) years of our country? Or is it individualism that produces isolation and tears the fabric of group loyalties apart? We wonder how extensively public policy can protect the individual without harming the group.

Other changes frighten most thinking people. Crime and drug use have discourteously left the street and entered respectable homes. At one time we could worry about getting robbed on the street, but now we know that white-collar criminals costs us more than masked and armed hoodlums. The U.S. government estimates that white-collar crime costs us as much as 44 billion dollars a year.[4] These criminals are our neighbors. Drugs used to be confined to dark alleys and awful people. Now the users are having parties centered on cocaine, and they are our friends and relatives.

The mass media and music industry are the most pervasive influences in our society. The movies that are being produced and becoming box office hits are not rated G. In fact, G-rated movies are few and far between. As for the rest of them, they prove that violence, nakedness, and horror are not just the words of a crazed preacher anymore. They are the selling points listed in the movie section of the local newspaper. The triple-X movies were always around—around the corner at the sleazy "art" theater. Now they are run on videocassette recorders in the home. Television, now on in the average home more than seven hours a day, reflect these trends. The television plots and language are like the bar talk of twenty years ago. Cable fare expands old censorship limits unchecked by anything but public opinion. Off the streets and into the homes march new models of previously hidden immorality.

One doesn't have to be a Christian to be frightened by this kind of freedom. In a 1986 Gallup survey concerning traditional values in matters of sex, morality, family life, and religion, the results were on the other end of the spectrum from society's trends. While the media are becoming more and more liberal, 36 percent of the nation's population saw their values as very traditional, 52 percent saw their values as moderate and only 11 percent saw their values as liberal! For Protestants the figures varied little (41 percent, 51 percent, and 7 percent respectively). When trends and values differ, one of the results is apprehension. And where should Americans turn with apprehensions about a fast-changing society? The natural answer is that they turn to religion (for old-fashioned values) and to politics (to put the brakes on society's permissiveness). Many are afraid that if both religion and government don't set up firmer standards, America will be like the man who fell into the vat of lanolin—and softened to death. Christians think of an even worse fate than that.

So enter the New Right Religious-Political Coalition. Their certainty and simple answers sound so—well, certain and simple. The certainty and simplicity give us a feeling of returning to basic morality. There is enough Christianity in our country's history to make it a significant component of our heritage and identity. But history, like Scripture, is open to a variety of interpretations. Several Christian authors have distilled American history in a way that ferments a potent theological statement. In many ways we Christians are thirsty to hear that America has merely "lost her way." We would love to accept the illusion that the ambiguity of this present culture is correctable, that complexity is just simplicity in big words. In our personal need for security and certainty, we are tempted to assume that what is best for our group is best for the entire nation.

In some respects right-wing political involvement has much in common with old wine. Internalized, it diminishes somewhat the pain of confusion and makes one feel brave and confident. There are certain ailments of our government that could do with a dose of right-wing involvement. But more than a little of such an influence diminishes capacity. Our body politic was not made to ingest strong, specific religious cures. And the New Testament does not recommend such an overwhelming infusion of Christianity into government.

The Old Testament–New Testament Confusion

One characteristic of evangelicals is their enthusiasm to search the entire Word of God (the Bible) to speak to every situation. According to Paul, "All Scripture is inspired by God and profitable for teaching, for reproof, for correction, for training in righteousness" (2 Tim. 3:16). And so it is. Yet not every part of the Bible has the same relevance to every situation. Amazingly, some students of the Bible miss the obvious difference between God's way of governing before Christ and His plan after Christ.

God used political leadership for people who were given His law. It was appropriate for Israel's maturing process, just as rules and parental force are appropriate for young children. The Scripture clearly states, though, that God was preparing them for another form of government. This would be one that would operate from the inside. Jeremiah 31:31, 33 prophesies this new government: "'Behold, days are coming,' declares the Lord, 'when I will make a new covenant. . . . I will put My law within them, and on their heart I will write it.'" Evangelicals believe that many Jews could not conceive of such a radically new system. The basic assumption among many evangelicals is that a strong reason the Jews do not accept Jesus as the Messiah is because He did not bring political change. These are the same evangelicals who, after they have called the Jews ignorant, are wanting Christ to reign politically!

The confusion comes with the Puritan tradition that assumes America to be the New Israel, a "city set on a hill," as John Winthrop so inspiringly stated. That Old Testament, "new chosen people" imagery might be good for ego gratification, but it is poor exegesis and silly theology. There was, and always will be, only one chosen people. God used Old Testament Israel for his special purposes, to be a blessing to all nations by preparing the world for the grace brought in

Christ. God needs no "new Israels." We are His people, not a revised version of the Jews. We are under no compulsion to imitate the government of Old Testament Israel.

God once ruled Israel by law and external government. God now rules His people by grace and internal government. John 1:17 states, "For the law was given through Moses; grace and truth were realized through Jesus Christ."

The New Testament does speak to the issue of Christians and government. We are to respect the external government: "Let everyone be in subjection to the governing authorities" (Rom. 13:1). We are to cooperate and give our civil duty its due: "Render to Caesar the things that are Caesar's" (Mark 12:17). We are to do such to aid our witness, our influence for Christ. First Peter 2:12-17 is quite clear about our obeying government so that others will see no wrong and "glorify God." But there is no implication in the New Testament that political reform, much less holding an office, should be a major part of our Christian strategy to share Christ with the world.

But wait! Some will protest that political strategy was not an option in New Testament times. They will say that democracy is such a new form of government that the New Testament does not speak to it. Let us explore the nature of our democracy and of our evangelical Christianity. We will see if they can be combined to operate as two parts in one strategy.

Democracy and Evangelical Christianity

Government can loosely be defined as a system of operation for a community of people. The following statements will be limited more specifically to the civil government of the United States of America. The definition will serve to illustrate that democracy and Christianity are very different organisms. They may cooperate with great results, but they may not be organically combined without profoundly confusing both.

Citizenship in the United States is a right of birth. Unlike Christianity, one becomes a member of the state before one understands the responsibilities of citizenship. Compulsory education in this country was established because of the recognized need to be capable of responsible citizenship. Democracy, literally meaning "the people ruling," in our country is based upon universal suffrage. That is, every individual has an equal unit of power—the vote. In contrast to the rule of a people by a sovereign God, the United States government is simply a way for people to rule themselves. God derives His power from who He is; our government derives its "just power from the consent of the governed."

When those two dynamics get switched or confused, problems begin. When, for example, a church becomes an institution where people are simply ruling themselves instead of trying to discern the dictates of God, the church loses its true identity. On the other hand, when people in a democracy only receive the dictates of government and refuse to try to improve those policies, democracy loses its true identity. The basis of the church is the recognized authority of God; the basis of democracy is the recognized authority of the people. Our government is made to vary with the people; religion is not. The philosopher Montesquieu, from whom our government borrowed the principle of the separation of powers, wrote, "It is the nature of human laws . . . to vary in proportion as the will of man changes; on the contrary, by the nature of the laws of religion, they are never to vary. Human laws appoint for some good; those of religion for the best; good may have another object because there are many kinds of good; but the best is but one; it cannot therefore change."[5]

The purposes of our civil government and of evangelical Christianity are also very different. In the Declaration of Independence, Thomas Jefferson wrote the assumption we as a nation have adopted. Government is the device by which we secure individual rights, "that among these are life, liberty, and the pursuit of happiness. That, to secure these rights, governments are instituted. . . ." The preamble to our Constitution develops these components further, directing that we as a group need to guard those individual opportunities to "form a more perfect union, establish justice, insure domestic tranquility, provide for the common defense, promote the general welfare, and secure the blessing of liberty to ourselves and our posterity." Our government is concerned with the order of the group so that the individual may prosper. That is also its function according to the New Testament (1 Tim. 2:1-2): "First of all, then, I urge that entreaties and prayers, petitions and thanksgivings, be made on behalf of all men, for kings and all who are in authority, in order that we may lead a tranquil and quiet life in all godliness and dignity." So protective order is the main function of our government. It may be said here that, historically and philosophically, one of its great vulnerabilities has been in its expansion of power, both domestically and in foreign endeavors. Democracy is strongest when not empire building. We have learned that while we cannot be isolated from the rest of the world, neither can we afford the mentality that says "conquer or be conquered." The wars involved in such expansion subtract liberty from our nation as well as the nations we would seek to control. Alexander Hamilton wrote in *The Federalist*, "The violent destruction of life and property incident to war, the continual danger, will compel nations the most attached to liberty to resort for repose and security to institutions which have a tendency to destroy their civil and political rights. To be more safe, they at length become willing to run the risk of being less free."[6]

Evangelical Christianity has a good part of its purpose in expanding. The second part of the scriptural quote that affirms the difference in purpose continues in this way: "This is good and acceptable in the sight of God our Savior, who desires all men to be saved and to come to the knowledge of the truth" (1 Tim. 2:3-4). The word *evangelical* comes from the combination of the Greek prefix *eu-*, meaning "good," and the word *angelos*, "a messenger." An evangelical, then, is one whose purpose it is to bring good news. Traditionally, as bearers of good news, Christians want others to respond by believing the news and committing their lives to God. That is expansionism pure and simple. Unlike our government, however, it is expansionism by individual agreement. A basic difference between our government and evangelical Christianity is the contrast in concerns. Our government is concerned with the group, so that the individual may prosper. Christianity is concerned with the individual, so that the group may prosper. We have defined government as a system of operation for a community of people. Perhaps it would not be too farfetched to begin defining evangelical Christianity as a system of operation for an individual in a community of people. The concern of government is to regulate one's relationship to fellow citizens. The concern of evangelical Christianity is to lift that neighbor to God.

The methods of civil government and evangelical Christianity are so different that to confuse them would be disastrous. Essentially, we granted our government the power to use force to insure compliance. Essentially, God granted our religion only the power of influence to insure compliance. Our government concerns itself with our proper behavior; hence the threat of force is appropriate, since force can moderate behavior. But Christianity's concern is the heart, or attitude, thinking, and will of a person. In such a deep realm, only faith is effective. The political philosopher Montesquieu said it well: "The influence of religion proceeds from its being believed; that of human laws from their being feared."[7]

Right Wing, Wrong Bird?

The religious right in politics have many admirable qualities. The right-wing activists are zealous, and we all respect that. These are no wishy-washy, milksop boys and girls. These are firebrands! The question, though, is not, How valuable is religious zeal in religion? The question is, How valuable is religious zeal in government? More exactly, it could be, Can religious zeal be valuable *to* government without being valuable *in* government?

The activists are practical (James 1:22) and sincere. They have a ring of certainty that is attractive. Their involvement is an act of integrity on their part. Yet for all those endearing qualities, they are missing a most important one: discernment. They have failed to discern the difference in the nature of a political system and the nature of Christianity. They have failed to discern the difference between established law and sacred law. They have also failed to discern the difference between acting responsibly toward certain issues (which Scripture specifically demands) and building a platform for political evangelism (which Scripture in no way recommends). It is not good to sew (cross-stitch?) the sacred onto a system governed by the people.

The biblical symbol for the Spirit is the dove (Matt. 3:16), traditionally associated with winsome qualities like grace, innocence, and purity. The national symbol for the U.S. is the bald eagle, traditionally associated with qualities like independence, strength, and majesty. Their qualities are certainly diverse and in many ways complementary. Yet we will show that transferring evangelical Christianity onto our system of government would alter the structure of both and be a major mistake—no wiser than transplanting the wing of a dove onto the shoulder of an eagle.

Notes

1. *Religion in America, 50 Years 1935–1985*, Gallup Report No. 236, May 1985.
2. William Bole, et al., *Present Tense*, Winter 1985, 24.
3. Rodney Stark and Bruce D. Foster, *Wayward Shepherds: Prejudice and the Protestant Clergy* (New York: Harper, 1970), 103.
4. David Toole, "Why the Boss Steals," *Maclean's*, 30 June 1986, 22.
5. Charles de Montesquieu, *The Spirit of Laws*, vol. 38, *Great Books of the Western World* (Chicago: Encyclopedia Britannica, 1952), 214-215.
6. Alexander Hamilton, *American Federalist Papers*, vol. 43, *Great Books of the Western World* (Chicago: Encyclopedia Britannica, 1952), 45.
7. Montesquieu, 215.

T W O

Thinkers or Tinkers? Doing Away with Naivete

The Bible teaches that no one—not the humanist, not the revolutionary, not even the most prestigious evangelical—is impervious to a contaminated self. One reason why many persons think sin is to be found mostly in society—notably in political institutions, social structures, and multinational corporations—is that they no longer sufficiently probe their own lives to admit where sin is really to be found.

Carl F. H. Henry

Evangelicals say the darndest things. If we were being interviewed by Art Linkletter on the subject of how to fix the American political system, we might well get a few laughs quite unintentionally. When trying to produce thinkers' thoughts, we say things that sound like answers. But heard on a higher level, they are tinkers' talks. Tinkers are those who putter ineffectively while trying to mend something. They are sincere but naive. We will examine five oft-heard evangelical answers to political problems. In the process of such examination we will call upon a few of the greatest thinkers in Western civilization to give us counsel of caution. Proverbs 12:15 states, "The way of a fool is right in his own eyes, but a wise man is he who listens to counsel."

"It's High Time the Majority Had Its Way in This Country"
Many in the majority of this country feel their rights are being violated by the rights of the minority. When, for example, an accused criminal is released from the legal process by a technicality, people feel the majority is endangered. When Affirmative Action rules that an employer be especially sensitive to the advantage of nonwhite men, there is anger. When Christians cannot express their faith in traditional public ways because the ACLU is slowly challenging all those public traditions, they feel frustrated.

Then this tinker-talk solution is thrown down like a gauntlet, daring anyone to refute its logic. "This is a democracy," people say, "where the majority rules." The "might makes right" answer sounds like it can shore up the slow loss of privilege that the majority has had for so long. Note the words of the philosopher of our Constitution, James Madison: "Wherever the real power in a government lies, there is the danger of oppression. In our government the real power lies in the majority of the community."[1]

Our Constitution basically agrees with our evangelical view of people. Evangelicals and the framers of the Constitution would agree that all people are self-centered, acting in self-interest. The Constitution, unlike Christianity, does not even try to change human nature. The Constitution is interested only in working, by checks and balances, to keep all factions in their proper places. Our government is structured to keep any faction (see Federalist Paper Number 10), including the majority, from becoming too powerful. Our government does not believe that any power group, including the majority, will naturally refrain from lording it over other groups. So most of our freedoms come from negatives—things we cannot do—so they cannot be done to us. Thus we are sensitized to others by institutions. The legal system insures that majority power can be dominant without being lethal.

It is strange to link evangelicals to a self-interested majority that needs to be held in check as all other factions do After all, we evangelicals are supposed to be sensitive and caring.

The Scriptures speak of serving. They say, "Do nothing from selfishness or empty conceit, but with humility of mind let each of you regard one another as more important than himself; do not merely look out for your own personal interests, but also for the interests of others" (Phil. 2:3-4). Yet where politics are concerned we have little or no evidence that evangelicals are any more sensitive to others' rights than any other interest group is. It is understandable. We have this Great Commission to win the world. That makes our zeal understandable, but also, possibly, dangerous. Moderation is the counsel, and if any group will not muster it themselves, the Constitution will muster it for them.

"We've Got to Win the Battle against Secular Humanism"
This truism isn't mere tinker talk—it is rooted in fact. Yet the *presentation* of the fact is all wrong. In an effort to work up intensity, evangelicals turn to the language of war. Realizing that there is a spiritual warfare (Eph. 6:10-18), we have transferred the concept to our earthly battle against the "secular humanists," those who hold man and not God as the measure and center of all things. The language used by evangelical alarmists conjures up images of conspiracy and attack. The residue of such war language is a tendency toward counterattack. Evangelicals feel persecuted by this menacing, hungry, secular humanist monster.

A word of caution and counsel comes from seventeenth-century political philosopher Charles de Montesquieu: "It is a principle that every religion that is persecuted becomes itself persecuting; for as soon as by some accidental turn it arises from persecution, it attacks the religion which persecuted it; not as religion, but as tyranny."[2] While we might argue the concept of "accidental turn"—certainly it is no accident that Christianity came to be the great religion that it is—we understand the danger Montesquieu speaks of. Evangelicals generally believe that secular humanism is a religion; religion can be defined in Paul Tillich's term of *ultimate concern*. Some evangelicals stretch their belief that secular humanists are persecuting us all by conspiratorial intention. In reality, the majority of secular humanists don't even know they are such. They are not only a great field for evangelism, they are just folks going along with the program of the world. It is neither appropriate nor effective to attack "them" as people trying to do Christians in. In *The Decline and Fall of the Roman Empire*, historian Edward Gibbon recorded that Emperor Julian had "artfully fomented the religious war" to the end that the "Christians had forgotten the spirit of the Gospel, and the pagans had imbibed the spirit of the church."[3]

Attack language aimed at people is just, well, offensive. There is real danger in secular humanistic philosophy, but the evangelicals' appropriate response should be to speak the truth in love. The attack language is counterproductive; it incites escalation in hate and smothers any witness to a world in need of "a more excellent way."

"We Ought to Go Back to the Good Old Days When Christians Ran Things"

History is not sure there were those good old days, and even if there were, it would not be an advancement to go back. History has one counsel for proceeding with Christian-led government: caution.

When Gibbon wrote *The Decline and Fall of the Roman Empire*, he had insight into weaknesses occasioned by the Christian emperors. The conflict between "civil and ecclesiastical" jurisdiction complicated the operations of government. When Emperor Constantine became a Christian in the year 313, he merged what had been two distinct and separate institutions in society. Matters changed. As the church gained favor in the courts, the Christians took these favors to be their "just and inalienable rights" instead of luxuries afforded by the times. As Constantine revealed his new faith, he earnestly exhorted his subjects to imitate him. With a veneer of moderation, he promised that all paganism could continue undisturbed. Then in a covert manner he undermined the safety of their ceremonies with legal technicalities. His sons followed his example "with more zeal and less discretion . . . every indulgence was shown to the illegal behavior of the Christians; every doubt was explained to the disadvantage of paganism."[4] The chance for the Christian emperors to become embroiled in religious controversies was consistently available and regularly indulged. Gibbon notes, for example, that Emperor Justinian often sacrificed the duty of father of his country to the role of defender of the faith.[5]

Not only emperors, but clergy have diminished stature in politicoreligious governments. Philosopher Thomas Hobbes observed the negative correlation between political powers and religious influence. His counsel was that we are not to be like those who "by too much grasping let go all." He saw the diminishing of religious leadership because "the pomp of them that obtained therein the principle public charges became by degrees so evident that they lost the inward reverence due to the pastoral function."[6] In other words, power and prestige corrupted what had been the formerly sacred office of pastor.

The church has suffered the subtraction of power resulting from its leaders' political ambitions. German philosopher Georg Wilhelm Hegel wrote, "What Popes acquired in point of land and wealth and direct sovereignty, they lost in influence and consideration. . . . The Church was no longer a spiritual power, but an ecclesiastical one; and the relation which the secular world sustained to it was unspiritual, automatic, and destitute of independent insight and conviction."[7]

Yes, but what about when Christians were running America? When was that? The amount of religious devotion within the hearts of our Founding Fathers is something only God knows. History, like Scripture, is open to interpretation. Atheists believe the Founding Fathers were just deists or adherents of some other "God is not actively involved in the world" religion. We Christians tend to look upon every religious reference the Fathers made as their truest, deepest rudder for life.

The truth probably lies somewhere in the middle. Both deism and Christianity were strong influences on the men who molded the policies of the new America.

We do know that the scenario of Christians benevolently and efficiently "running things" for America didn't really happen in the past. We like the image, but it isn't real, nor should it have been. Dean Inge said once, "Like certain ministers of state, the Church has always done well in opposition, and badly in office." That is the sobering word of caution we should include in any romantic notion of Christians running things in the good old days.

"We Can Fix Things If We Elect Evangelicals"

The game plan for more Christian influence in government includes a rather simplistic notion: the qualifications for office are predominantly spiritual ones. We know that Article Six of the Constitution states "no religious test shall ever be required as a qualification to any office or public trust under the United States." But that only applies to a government test, not an individual evaluation, right? Yes, but the deeper issue attached to the notion of "qualification" is relevant here. The Founding Fathers sensed that a person's religion should not be a major issue in being qualified. Some people are trying to change that. In fact, evangelicals face the temptation of so focusing on a candidate's faith that other qualifications seem secondary. Tim LaHaye is the president of a large politico-evangelical umbrella group in America, the American Coalition for Traditional Values (ACTV). In an ACTV pamphlet entitled *Has the Church Been Deceived?* LaHaye is quoted as saying, "At this crucial time in history, every Christian should do one or the other—run for office or help someone else run." But if Christians are to run for office, they need other qualifications than holiness.

In an age of specialization we must understand the need for specific knowledge and skill as well as foundational faith. To operate effectively in our political system we must have more than a general knowledge of how government works, or should work. Experience is critical in separating the real from the ideal. Experience is critical in building relationships necessary for group effort. Experience is critical in building long-lasting teams of trustworthy subordinates. Often officials are not sabotaged by their own mistakes but by the mistakes of those that surround them. So even if evangelicals can quickly master the new technology of the field—in media campaigning, computer-targeting constituency subgroupings, etc.—government is still an unknown skill to an amateur.

Before Christ, Plato attacked amateurism in government. In both *The Republic* and *The Statesman*, he held fast to the principle that one's expert capabilities constituted one's right to govern. In *The Republic* he outlined an ideal training program for philosopher-rulers that began in early childhood and was not completed until the age of fifty! While Plato's social vision and his training program are not those of a participatory democracy, his point should not be lost. Governing is a serious matter. Those who desire to rule need to have demonstrated competence in the field before they are thrust into responsibility for governing. Plato's pupil Aristotle said it this way: "If therefore, there is anyone superior in virtue and in the power of performing the best actions, him we ought to follow and obey, but he must have the capacity for action as well as virtue."[8]

"We Don't Have to Force Our Religion, Just Be Able to Express It"

A thinker's thought: Institutional expression is not without force. As has been mentioned, the power of government and its various institutions is force. The power of Christianity is persuasion. Any and all activities carried on by governmental institutions can't help but convey the force linked with government authority. Any Christian activity expressed by a governmental institution insinuates force. To believe otherwise is amazingly naive. We Christians have had the luxury of special niches within our government for years. We are now only beginning to realize what privilege we have had. Maybe we will keep them. But if we do, it would be silly to say that those expressions do not influence others' freedom.

Additionally, what exactly are we saying about expression without force? Are we saying that we can water it down so much that it will not be forceful? Are we saying that prayer in school or the chaplain in Congress is there for decorative purposes only? John Stuart Mill, the nineteenth-century political philosopher, wrote of this type of religious window dressing: "The demand [is] now so general in England for having the Bible taught, at the option of pupils or their parents, in the government schools. From the European point of view nothing can wear a fairer aspect or seem less open to objection on the score of religious freedom. To Asiatic eyes it is quite another thing. No Asiatic people ever believes that a government puts its paid officers and official machinery into motion unless it is bent on an object; and when bent on an object, no Asiatic believes that any government, except a feeble and contemptible one, pursues it by halves."[9] Children have Asiatic eyes, and so do most of us. We discern a purpose in any modeled behavior, then hold it in contempt if it is only half-pursued. The notion of institutional expression without force is at once attractive and repugnant. Lip service has always been good manners with little meaning. And our Lord always criticized those who were lukewarm.

There is also a feeling in the phrase "just be able to express it" that gives us the feeling that we are guarding or protecting Christianity. If we can just tinker with it by saying a general prayer in school or putting a nativity scene on the courthouse lawn, we feel we are fending off the infidels. But protection is not our object in the faith—evangelism is! When we reduce Christianity to something we can protect, we have lost all perspective of the sovereignty of God. He is in charge here, regardless of the laws. As John Locke wrote, "Christ . . . prescribed . . . no peculiar form of government . . . the Truth certainly would do well enough if she were once left to shift for herself. She is not taught by laws, nor has she any need of force to procure her entrance into the minds of men . . . if the

Truth makes her entrance into the minds of men . . . if the Truth makes not her way into the understanding by her own light, she will be but the weaker for any borrowed force violence can add to her."[10] Locke was the philosopher our Founding Fathers looked to for their concept of religious toleration. His words of counsel here lead us to question how much government can protect Christian traditions without our substituting protection for Christian growth.

After the Platitudes

All five platitudes discussed above have some truth in them. That is why they are so popular and they strike such a chord within us. We wish the solutions were as simple and clear as those platitudes sound. In fact, it is not a simple matter to think our way to what really helps the Christian cause. Even with the help of Scripture to remind us of our purpose and to give us counsel on our attitudes, the issues are still complex. Einstein once said, "Politics is more difficult than physics." Amen. But we can know a few things about thinking Christianity in politics.

First, we are called to be involved in government but not to depend upon it for solutions. The Christian right seeks support in government. It could be irony, judgment, or God's great sense of humor that finds the conservatives now doing what they accused the liberals of doing for years—looking to government for solutions. We may get an answer, but they will never get a solution. It is the nature of government to make matters more complicated. Government finds, as science does, that every answer raises more questions. Nevertheless, government is such an intricate part of our lives we cannot avoid it. When the evangelical cares about his neighbor in practical ways, participation at the polls must be a part of that caring. Like it or not, government has an effect on the poor and the elderly. Like it or not, issues of justice and freedom for people are the business of government. If we want justice for our neighbor, we must insure it by participation.

Second, we are called to be involved not only by implication but by Christ directly. When He said, "Render to Caesar the things that are Caesar's" (Matt. 22:21), He was telling us to respond to government's requests of us. Our government requests participation of all citizens, including evangelicals. So we obey Christ.

Finally, our government requests participation of all citizens and special interest groups—and make no mistake about it, evangelical Christianity is a special interest group—for a specific reason. Our Founding Fathers envisioned a balance of power through healthy competition. They believed what would control each segment of society and advance society as a whole was the dynamic of the segments vying for dominance. If evangelicals do not participate with their perspective and power, they rob the American system. They also rob the American people of exposure to and the influence of the Christian perspective. American politics are competitive and complicated, but politics provides one of God's great ways of maturing our thinking and testing our commitment.

Notes

1. Richard Hofstadter, *American Political Tradition* (New York: Vintage, 1948), 3.
2. Charles de Montesquieu, *The Spirit of Laws*, vol. 38, *Great Books of the Western World* (Chicago: Encyclopedia Britannica, 1952), 211.
3. Edward Gibbon, *The Decline and Fall of the Roman Empire*, vol. 40, *Great Books*, 382.
4. Ibid., 329.
5. Gibbon, vol. 41, 148.
6. Thomas Hobbes, *Leviathan*, vol. 23, *Great Books*, 276.
7. Georg Wilhelm Friedrich Hegel, *Philosophy of History*, vol. 46, *Great Books*, 331.
8. Aristotle, *Politics*, vol. 9, *Great Books*, 529.
9. John Stuart Mill, *Representative Government*, vol. 43, *Great Books*, 438.
10. John Locke, *A Letter Concerning Toleration*, vol. 35, *Great Books*, 15.

THREE

Rev. President: The Search for a Political Saint

A good government remains the greatest of human blessings, and no nation has ever enjoyed it.

William R. Inge

It will be most interesting in future elections to see how religious leaders of celebrity status are coaxed to run for political office. To some evangelicals "'tis a consummation devoutly to be wished." The transference from religious authority to political authority might be quite natural for some Christians. The normative way to effect representation is to send a leader instead of the whole company.

Yet there is a broader issue here. How could a significant number of American people be serious about a candidate whose credentials are concentrated in religious leadership? Part of the answer lies in several cultural developments that may open the door for a "Christian ticket" in subsequent elections. Let us look now at those cultural factors, then at religious factors that would contribute to such a possibility.

Authorities and Authority

American history is like a family photo album. We can see and remember the important people in our lives. We can understand our present outlooks by deciphering their impression upon us. We can also see certain recurring traits woven throughout the generations.

The presidents we elect are the important people in our political lives. Their personalities reflect our current needs. They, in turn, make an impression on us. They set a precedent in our perception of what is acceptable in a candidate and what needs to be avoided in a candidate. Our reactions to past presidents have much to do with who we elect in the future.

The recurring trait we can see in our American family album is our love-hate relationship with authority. We alternately seek it and rebel against it. We build security under it, then we desire freedom that security always threatens to stifle. From our beginning as a nation we desired freedom from the control of our mother country England, so we fought for independence. Then we had, in the place of the mother country, a loosely confederated group of colonies. Then we had a union of states with states' rights. Then we had a union with a balance of federal and state powers. Then we had—surprise!—another strong federal government. But we love that strong federal government, don't we? Yes and no. We love the security it offers and hate its control over our lives.

There may have been a time in our history when the president and the federal government were seen as one source of authority. If there ever was, it is gone, and our affection for each is much diminished. In recent years we have begun to deal with this love-hate relationship with authority by dividing our affections between the person of the president in whom we hope and the big government we resent. We can rather easily trace the development of this mentality.

Falling Out of Love with Authority

In the 1950s we tended to love security. We remember those years somewhat like the TV series "Happy Days" portrayed them. We elected a general in successive landslide victories. "I like Ike," we said. And we did like Ike. He was a father figure representing stability and security. Though he was a military man, he was anything but warlike in office. He was dignified and genial, avoiding tacky conflicts in Congress. He was patient and tolerant when attacked by radical McCarthy elements. He was suspicious of the expanding role of government and restrained in his use of executive power. And *he* was loved. He could not transfer the public's affection to his party, nor bequeath it to his vice-president (Nixon) in the 1960 election. Yet the public's affection for the president and the institution of government was not yet fully split. We had not yet put our confidence, as differentiated from our affection, in a man. We were still institutionalized. That is to say, we put much faith in our institutions of government, mainline churches, work places, and family. That is where our loyalty (remember that word?) was solidly set, for awhile anyhow. Only a small number of curiosities, called "beatniks," foreshadowed the anti-establishment era to come. There were a few weird singers around, like one Elvis (the pelvis) Presley, but we knew they would never match the likes of Perry Como and Lawrence Welk.

In the 1960 presidential election America surprised herself. John F. Kennedy was a young idealist who made an altar call. His was the patriotism that called Americans beyond security under government to consecration of service: "Ask not what your country can do for you, ask what you can do for your country." Kennedy's charisma was evident in its time and hallowed in memory. The problem was, of course, that the vision was more inspiring than defined. We felt like we had a fistful of promise, and when he was shot we were left with just the fist. It felt as if we had placed our confidence in Kennedy as a man, and now he was gone. Without our leader, things quickly disintegrated. President Johnson tried to carry on the only way he knew how—legislate improvement. There were more civil rights bills and social programs passed in his "Great Society" than in all of Kennedy's dreams, but no one paid attention. The baby boomer generation was disenchanted with institutional government. The campus dwellers, vaccinated against authority by educator John Dewey's pen, came apart. The ideal of peace was mocked by the violent demonstrations for it. The two leaders who could have had some moderating effect were killed in 1968. Martin Luther King, Jr., and Robert Kennedy died just two months apart.

By the time Richard Nixon was elected in 1968, our culture was frightened by freedom. The young people—and many who were not so young—were trampling all traditional forms of security, or at least had left them. Institutional loyalty was gone. "Letting it all hang out" was here. Morality was not yet so much the issue—survival was. Now security—"law and order"—looked good.

Richard Nixon, because of his experience and longevity on the political scene, seemed the safest choice. Here was a man who spoke to our fears and was trusted by virtue of his seniority in government. In a few years we would connect seniority in government with *lack* of virtue. The sense of chaos continued when both Nixon and Agnew, after promising law and order, had to leave office for illegal activities. Nixon was supposed to make us secure; he made us mad. We had had enough of polluted big government.

Carter was clear of corruption. We put our confidence in his character. This man was a born-again Christian and not afraid to say it. But while we were getting used to having a president intimately connected with his faith, we also had to endure a president constantly overrun by circumstances beyond his control. His presidency was deflated by inflation and held hostage by Iran. He was the Charlie Brown of Pennsylvania Avenue. Every time he went to kick the football, somebody moved it. But he was a good man, and we admired his intentions.

So bring on the old cowboy-soldier-sports announcer. What a guy. He shot down inflation, captured a working strategy with Congress (who read the polls), and supported legislation that made conservatives cheer. We developed confidence in his ability as well as his character. And he did it all while befriending the new political religious right.

So then, we have been brought to a point in our history

where we are bored by, but attracted to, old "Happy Days" (Eisenhower). We have linked inspiration to the presidency (Kennedy). We are disgusted with inveterate Washington corruption (Nixon). We have become accustomed to religion in the White House (Carter). We are able to connect competence and popularity with the support of evangelical issues (Reagan). An evangelical religious leader running for president should not be such a surprise to us. Americans who want to love a president and resist big government will continue to be attracted to Washington outsiders. Americans who want to get back to the basics will find religion attractive. Americans who want to elevate morality to a higher level than they are themselves committed to living will naturally entertain the idea of a religious leader ticket. And there is more. We have yet to see the full potential of the most powerful cultural aid to a candidate for president.

Television: Now You See It, Now You Vote

Before the advent of television, the chances of having a non-politician as a viable candidate for a top office would have been virtually nil. The American two-party system, like most systems, was one of "working your way up through the ranks." The system still requires that to some degree, but voters don't. Before television we would vote on the candidates produced by party caucus and convention. The odds of a rookie candidate greatly influencing the direction of the political party: next to none. Television has changed all that.

Charles McDowell remembers television's impact on the 1952 Republican convention. In a most interesting article on television politics, he reports an interparty argument resolved on the basis of feedback from television audiences. People were telephoning and telegraphing their delegates to say how the sides were coming through on television. "Up to now in the debate, the Taft spokesmen had tended to be the crusty elders of the party. The Eisenhower spokesmen were somehow younger, trimmer, clearer of eye. To make their motion ... the Taft side passed over the elders and chose a young, clean-cut, well-spoken committee member. . . . Two days into the era of television politics, and everyone was beginning to catch on."[1] The Eisenhower persona as visible on the television, the article continues, went on to rise above party politics and even to draw millions from the other party. And television has been doing that for candidates ever since.

A new candidate can be plausible simply on the basis of positive exposure on television. In our world, much of which comes to us through the picture tube, visibility is prominence. Consistent visibility is credibility. Media adds power; it amplifies importance. Carpenter reports that in New Guinea, when a village leader is ignored by his people, his speech is recorded on tape and then played to the now respectful villagers.[2] In another setting he reports an overheard conversation. "Oh, what a beautiful baby!" "That's nothing," replied the mother. "You should see his photograph."[3] Media has a magnifying effect.

So what does that have to do with any religious leader who has a lot of media exposure—say, a weekly television show? Plenty. He not only has the automatic magnification of television, but he is esteemed because of his vocation. According to a 1985 Gallup survey of the public's perception of "honesty and ethical standards" in professions, clergy rank first. Of the twenty-five occupations listed, senators, congressmen, local political officeholders, and state political officeholders all rank in the lower half of the survey.[4] While there may be a difference in the esteem of a local clergyman and a television clergyman (the survey does not differentiate), the high regard conveys credibility. All of this evidence helps us answer the question of how "in the world" a religious leader could be considered a viable candidate. And there is more.

We have seen that television can virtually eliminate the middleman (the political party) in politics by providing direct access to the voter. We are now ready to consider the voter's reliance upon image rather than information. Our culture has switched so completely from a print medium (which relays information) to a visual-auditory medium (which relays impressions) that images are taken to be information. Like the Wizard of Oz, political candidates and other television personalities find it possible to project an image upon the screen that looms more powerful, competent, and wise than the real person. And like Toto the dog, television investigative reporters like running over and pulling away the curtain. But most people don't mind relying upon an image to answer their needs.

There is a downside and an upside to this television image dynamic. The downside is that we can never be sure if the real person is coming through. Perhaps what we see on television is a projection of who he really is and what he really means. Or perhaps he just has a smarter image consultant. In any case, we need to listen for his ideals and strategy and not just watch a staged event that relays an image.

The upside is that our attention to television can unify us as a nation. The image can give us consolidation with the president in ways that we feel are personal and, along with basic ideological consensus, can move us forward together. Reagan's popularity healed the nation in many ways that had nothing to do with the issues. Our political decisions should be made on an informed, thoughtful basis, yet a sense of unity with the personage can be an added benefit to us all.

Television has a third effect. Not only does it override party politics with personal visibility and dilute information with image, but television also tends to stimulate response over deliberation. Media specialist Tony Schwartz writes that media are no longer as concerned with conveying a message as with striking a responsive chord within people. He writes that television conditions people "to respond instantly to stimuli in their everyday lives ... by focusing people's attention on the current moment ... and we process new information instantly, rather than think out decisions."[5] Later he writes, "much sociological research today centers on cultural phenomena arising from an orientation toward the current fleeting moment. . . . It is more than curious that a society in which impulse control is a major problem, receives most of its information . . . in the form of television."[6]

Advertisers, politicians, and evangelical religious leaders often seek to stimulate a response rather than cause deliberation. That is not so shady as it may sound. Evangelical leaders, for example, are often speaking to the already converted. The converted do not always need new information as much as they need to be motivated to put into practice what they already know. (This is called *revival.*) Admittedly, evangelical leaders do not challenge people to think and reason often enough, but in a religious setting there is some validity to playing on the responsive chord. Presidents, too, have reason to pay attention to this need for the right chord. When Jimmy Carter complained of the "malaise" in America, he was searching in vain to strike a responsive chord. Like the little boy returning his harmonica to the store and saying, "Mister, I've blowed all up and down that thing and there just ain't no songs in it," Carter could have used a lesson in guiding his breath to the right chord. Such a quality is invaluable in the presidency.

The danger, of course, is one of persuasion without intellectual foundation. It is a danger both in the church and in the political system. It is a danger both in the speaker and in the audience. If we have been conditioned to act on impression rather than informed decision, if we feel more than we think, we are in danger of making short-lived commitments. A majority of Americans today vote on the basis of their impression of a candidate rather than on their attention to his stand on the important issues. According to Yale psychologist Robert Ableson, "Feelings are three or four times as important as issues."[7]

We need to pay attention to one final connection between TV candidacy and religion: money. Television has become *the* instrument for campaigning. The bills are staggering. McDowell writes, "Television, selling time for political advertising, has enhanced the power of money in politics beyond our prior imagining. The cost of campaigns—national, state and local—has risen astronomically as the television age has advanced. Reliance on special interests and single-issue zealots to finance campaigns has increased to the point of a clear and present danger and disgrace."[8]

Evangelical Christians constitute a special interest group—with money. This comes as no surprise. Religion has always been the major benefactor of benevolent giving in this country. According to a report of the American Association of Fund-Raising Counsel in the December 22, 1986, issue of *U.S. News & World Report*, private giving comes from individuals and goes to religion. While 83.5 percent (66 billion dollars) of benevolent giving comes from individuals, it is divided among a broad spectrum of causes. Out of all the spectrum, religion commanded a whopping 47.5 percent (38 billion dollars). The closest seconds are health and education causes with 13.75 percent (11 billion) each. Additionally, of all the volunteer work that saves expending money, 23 percent is done in religious work, followed by 13 percent in education and 10 percent in recreation. One can see the rich resources religion manages in this country.

The plain fact is that candidates—whether religious leaders, evangelical laymen, or mildly religious conservatives—pay attention to the religious right, hoping they can garner the attention that pays. Evangelicals are already in the posture of giving; it is built into their life-style to a large degree. So evangelicals have great potential in supporting a television campaign, which is not unlike supporting a television ministry. And the evangelical will see supporting a religious candidate as an aspect of practical Christianity. It is indeed.

Electing a Moses Figure to Capitol Hill

We have seen how a recognized religious leader could become a credible candidate for the office of president. Our national love-hate relationship with authority means that many people want strong leadership without big government. The precedents of presidents have made some evangelical

Christianity at home in the White House. Television has advanced the power of the popular person to circumvent traditional political party procedures. Strong evangelical leaders with TV exposure have a current cultural advantage. Now that the office is open to a recognized religious leader, what makes the possibility so attractive to evangelical Christians?

Many evangelicals believe that Christianity is facing eradication in governmental institutions. They also sense the expanding sphere of power of those institutions. Some people fear that governmental institutions intimidated by the American Civil Liberties Union will eradicate the influence of Christians. In comparison with the persecution of early Christians by the emperors, facing the ACLU is a picnic. Yet when the traditional Christian customs are questioned, there is fear among evangelical Christians. Extrapolation (inference of a future trend on the basis of a present fact) is a scary thing. It tends to carry one's imagination to logical extremes, and extremes cause a fearful reaction. One may not be shocked by the exclusion of organized prayer time in public schools, but link that exclusion with the government's desire to have a say in private Christian schools, and the imagination runs wild.

Many evangelicals believe religious freedom, if not religion itself, faces major problems with the government in the future. With special interest groups' rights movements and frequent individual's rights assertion, the "other side" has become aggressive. Lawsuits abound. People are wearing sweatshirts that read, *My lawyer can beat up your lawyer.* In such a situation, the tendency of many Christians is to try to use the government to mediate between an aggressive minority seeking freedom from religion and a Christian tradition seeking freedom in religion. By political ascendancy, Christians can influence the mediation (it's a dirty job, but somebody has to do it!). And what better way to gain ascendancy than to pick a champion of the cause, an upright evangelical father figure, for the top office of the land? He can influence legislation, appoint judges, and speak the cause. Can he? Or should he?

Exercising Responsibility to Avoid Responsibility

For evangelical Christians, this particular strategy has inherent dangers. The first danger is that electing a father figure is more often a way of avoiding responsibility than solving problems. The counsel of both science and Scripture is unified on this point.

Psychiatrist-author M. Scott Peck identifies three shortcomings that could become evident in our embracing this political strategy. The three are all well-known to us, in experience as well as observation. First, Peck notes, people have the inclination to avoid solving problems. We tend to look for a substitute for the legitimate work and pain of problem solving. Do the words "there must be an easier way" sound familiar? Of course, easier is not always better. The catch is that "the substitute itself ultimately becomes more painful than the legitimate suffering it was designed to avoid."[9] Yet we continue to look for ways out of the work that is ours to do.

Second, Peck observes that we have great difficulty even accepting responsibility for what we know to be our duty. This nonacceptance of responsibility is often activated after we have accepted the responsibility. What then do we do with it? "Whenever we seek to avoid the responsibility for our own behavior, we do so by attempting to give that responsibility to some other individual or organization or entity."[10]

The third shortcoming is the tendency we have toward transferring our childhood ways of dealing with the world to our adult lives. Peck's definition of transference is "that set of ways of perceiving and responding to the world which is developed in the childhood environment (indeed, often lifesaving) but which is inappropriately transferred into the adult environment." An example might be that we choose to let a political parent figure think for us and take care of us rather than to grow wise and competent ourselves.

These subtle tendencies named have appeared in the scriptural witness repeatedly. For evangelical Christians it is a familiar story, beginning in the Garden of Eden. Eve may well have seen the forbidden fruit's wisdom as an easier alternative to the normal work of life. Adam followed. When Adam (a Hebrew name for both the individual and the species of mankind) faced the consequences of his problem, rather than working out a solution with the God he faced, he quickly passed on the responsibility: "The woman whom Thou gavest to be with me, she gave me from the tree" (Gen. 3:12).

Eve also tried to avoid the responsibility: "The serpent deceived me." Since that time it has been our nature to try to avoid responsibility and avoid solving problems. We would rather shift the responsibility to someone else.

We also see the process of responsibility-shifting the Hebrew nation was forming. In its childhood stages, God gave to it great leaders, like Moses and Joshua. The nation responded to them in childlike ways: dependence and rebellion. And it was appropriate for that stage of development—indeed it was often lifesaving. For example, when the Hebrews were being persecuted in Egypt, God raised up a great leader—Moses. Moses (whose adoptive father was also a political figure) accepted the responsibility to lead the people out of persecution to the Promised Land. He was charged with going up and down the mountain as the intermediary with God: "Then they said to Moses, 'Speak to us yourself and we will listen; but let not God speak to us, lest we die'" (Exod. 20:19). And so the dependence developed. God, through Moses, gave the people direction, provisions, and law. There is little evidence that the people responded by growing up. In fact, the generation that first followed grumbled against him and never did get to enter the Promised Land. Even when we are immature there are consequences to be paid for rebellion. Yet the point is that there was a time when strong political leadership was appropriate in the journey of God's people. However, we cannot justifiably transfer that method of operation to the present. The New Testament calls us to grow up in our political style.

The difference between the Old Testament and the New

Testament approaches to civil government is infinite. The New Testament approach will be addressed later. The point to be made here is that it is not any great leader's responsibility to solve the Christians' problems. Though leaders were appointed for order in the church (1 Tim. 3), no passage in the New Testament encourages Christians to appoint for themselves a political leader. The leader Christ gives to us to help us speak our cause to the world is the Holy Spirit (John 16:13), not a fallible, flesh-and-blood political leader. The Bible makes it clear that we are not to put too much faith in political leaders ("Do not trust in princes, in mortal man, in whom there is no salvation," Ps. 146:3).

We must avoid the temptation of political reliance on one person. It is possible for us to be involved in political action in more ways than electing another to do our job. The momentary (and easy) political act of voting for the "right" candidate can help us avoid continual personal responsibility. We can sit back and let President Christian turn the world around. Never mind that we ourselves have a responsibility for making the world a better place by modeling Christ in our lives.

We want a Christian leader who can help us avoid continual responsibility. He can keep watch on the government. He can influence legislation. He can be the spokesman for Christianity. He can defend us from creeping secular humanism. But he can't help us grow up politically.

And where did we get the idea that a president could turn the country around morally? We rightly want a good man, a man with sound morals, as president, but we can't expect something as massive as the federal government to undergo a total moral overhaul because the president happens to be a good man. Ocean liners don't stop on a dime, and nations don't become utopias because the head man has integrity and zeal. Four years is a short time to turn a country into a God-centered state. In fact, it can't be done in four hundred years. We can't be so naive—and both conservatives and liberals are guilty of this—that we believe the right man in the White House will solve all problems. No one can shoulder that burden. One person can only do so much good.

Electing a Moses figure to run up and down Capitol Hill for us could be an act of laziness if not cowardice. It overestimates the power of the presidency, underestimates the power of the average Christian activist, and lets us avoid the individual art of influence. It is a plus to elect a president who happens to be an evangelical Christian. It is a minus to elect a recognized religious leader as our political Savior and expect that he will bring about heaven on earth.

Notes

1. Charles McDowell and Paul Duke, eds., *Beyond Reagan: The Politics of Upheaval* (New York: Warner, 1986), 239.
2. Ted Carpenter, *They Became What They Beheld* (New York: Ballantine, 1970), n.p.
3. Ibid.
4. Gallup Survey 255 Q 10a.
5. Tony Schwartz, *The Responsive Chord* (Garden City, N.Y.: Doubleday, 1974), 17.
6. Ibid., 158.
7. Robert Ableson, "Not by Issues Alone," *Time*, 12 November 1984, 37.
8. McDowell and Duke, 242.
9. M. Scott Peck, *The Road Less Traveled* (New York: Simon and Schuster, 1978), 17.
10. Ibid., 42.

FOUR

The Press in the Pews

For me personally the media have come to give off a whiff of sulfur, and yet at the end of the day I have to admit that they can enrich as well as debase a life.

Malcolm Muggeridge

No one but God has direct access to all the happenings of the world. We human beings, therefore, need a reporter if we desire any information outside the realm of our own experience. And not just any reporter will do. The quantity of information requires a reporter with a broad intake ability. The complexity of the information may require a reporter who has understanding of the area reported. And certainly at times the information cannot be conveyed with full meaning unless the reporter is sympathetic to it. In the communication process, a tone of voice or an arrangement of words can predispose the listener toward a perverted—or true—reception of information.

Today our reporters for world events are our national media journalists. The reporters for spiritual events are our spiritual leaders, or the religious media journalists. It has not always been so. There were times in frontier America when the church was our window to the world. In a country where farming was the main commerce, and neighbors were often miles away, church served as the center of socialization and information. The parson, who traveled if he had more than one church, brought news from surrounding communities. He usually was the most well-read, well-informed man around. His reports did not come as objective news. His reference point was the Bible he carried. In that Bible was a distinct accusation from our Lord about people who could interpret the world according to the world, but not according to the Spirit (Matt. 16:1-4). The parson did not want to be such a person.

Our Bible is a record of seeing God's hand in the events of history. It is a record that states we cannot be fully informed of events' content and meaning unless both the reporter and the listener have spiritual perception. Paul, in 1 Corinthians 2:13-15, states that the world cannot be reported or perceived "in words taught by human wisdom, but in those taught by . . . the Spirit of God; for they are foolishness to [the worldly man], and he cannot understand them, because they are spiritually appraised. But he who is spiritual appraises all things, yet he himself is appraised by no man." So the spiritual person, according to Scripture, may understand the spiritual meaning of world events. It is his responsibility to report objective events *and* their spiritual meaning. But the nonspiritual person does not understand, and therefore cannot report, spiritual insights. It is his job to stick to the objective events without attempting to convey things of a spiritual nature.

When these two reporters are switched in their agenda, as they will be more and more if religious leaders and political leaders are the same people, it makes one wonder what will happen. When the job of a religious leader is to report world events without their spiritual meaning, much will be lost. When the job of a reporter is to report the faith and the activities of Christians because politics has now made them "newsworthy," much will be perverted. And many could be turned away from the gospel, inoculated from the real message by a dead interpretation.

The Church Reporting on the World

The church's relations with the world are sometimes close, sometimes distant. For many Christians, the relationship to the world can become one of avoidance. In many evangelical churches the sermons and teachings are so isolated from the world's perspective that they could be just as relevant delivered on any planet in the solar system. As long as the sermons address God's people, it is assumed, the relevancy of others or the environment is questionable—until they are "blood" relation. In other words, what business does the church have with the outside world, that often malevolent realm?

To other believers the world is not ignored or avoided, but accepted. In many liberal mainline churches there is no distinction to be emphasized; Christians live in the world and are not notably different from non-Christians. In the liberal churches the guidance of the Bible and the Holy Spirit may not be emphasized. When spiritual matters are mentioned, the reply is, "Yeah, but I still live in this world." The newspaper can be as significant as the Bible, and sometimes more instructive.

Traditionally, liberal Christians have spoken to societal issues with a less distant perspective than the evangelical. (This hasn't always been true, but, for the most part, it has been true for much of this century.) When liberal Christians make pronouncements on political and social issues, they do not speak as holy outsiders, but as fellow citizens who happen to have religious beliefs. They generally choose to interpret the world using the standard that both the Bible and the world hold highest—love. Using this standard of interpretation, they report on the world, and the report is fully understandable to anyone who listens. The report is devoid of any exclusive terms—Christian jargon—that the listeners have to know. The interpretation of the world and faith is one of common sense and encouragement that calls people to change only in the most general ways, if at all. For these reasons, liberal Christians, both in our Founding Fathers' days and in ours, fit so much more easily into the political arena. Their vision of the world is not so distinctly spiritual that it would exclude the nonspiritual. Pure, unalloyed Christianity is willingly sacrificed for some practical impact. Eventually the Christ distinction becomes so "watered down" that it is indistinguishable from any other human perspective that has some general moral quality. And, until the recent upsurge in evangelical strength, few cared.

Christians can be nasty to each other. Liberal Christians have often accused evangelicals of being too idealistic and of using too much Christianese when addressing the world. They have claimed that evangelicals are out of touch with the pluralistic society in which they live. They have claimed that evangelicals emphasize prayer and Bible study to the neglect of active involvement in social concerns. Evangelicals have accused liberals of letting the world set the agenda for the church. They have said that liberals lose the full strength of the gospel because they have abandoned evangelism (which has a long-term goal—eternity) in favor of social change (which has only a short-term goal). Most important, they have accused liberals of losing a distinctively Christian perspective.

Scripture does say there is a much different mind-set than the world offers.

> This I say therefore, and affirm together with the Lord, that you walk no longer just as the Gentiles also walk, in the futility of their mind, being darkened in their understanding, excluded from the life of God, because of the ignorance that is in them, because of the hardness of their heart; and they, having become callous, have given themselves over to sensuality, for the practice of every kind of impurity with greediness. But you did not learn Christ in this way, if indeed you have heard Him and have been taught in Him, just as truth is in Jesus, that, in reference to your former manner of life, you lay aside the old self, which is being corrupted in accordance with the lusts of deceit,

> and that you be renewed in the spirit of your mind, and put on the new self, which in the likeness of God has been created in righteousness and holiness of the truth. Therefore, laying aside falsehood, speak truth, each one of you, with his neighbor. (Eph. 4:17-25)

According to Scripture, the Christian life is different from regular life. The Christian understanding is different. The Christian himself must be the reporter to his neighbor from the perspective of his new life. The subject matter of the report is not just the world improved. It is the radically new life of people reborn and remade.

That is the message (*evangel*) to be taken not only by all believers—well-known religious leaders included—to the world. Their responsibility to report God's purpose, the Spirit's action, Christ's work, Scripture's guidance to the world is not lessened by any circumstance, including political office. It is their job, as it is every Christian's job, to report what they are not ashamed of. As representatives of a distinct movement within history, evangelicals have already been elected (by God) to present a special way of life to people. America needs to decide if evangelical candidates can deliver their distinct vision and still represent the electorate. When the evangelical speaks to the world, then, he speaks from the Christian perspective—or he is a hypocrite. There can be no illusion of "objectivity." No Christian can flip a switch and be "worldly" at one moment and "religious" the next moment. A Christian who holds political office is always a Christian, and he always views the world through the lens of the Bible. Messengers from God have an agenda from God. It may be hidden or denied, but it is there. But while a Christian cannot be, strictly speaking, objective about the world, neither can people in the media.

The World Reporting on the Church

If evangelical leaders (reporters of God's views) should cast out the illusion of objectivity in their reporting to the world, perhaps the world should also examine itself in its own reporting objectivity. Certainly, the world should never presume to report on the spiritual activity of God in his church. Yet that is the very thing that the presence of Christians in politics drives the world to do. We need to take a careful look at what will happen when the world's reporters interpret spiritual concerns. We can see most clearly the implications of such a "cruci-fiction" when we look at the present nature of our national media.

I believe most reporters and broadcasters do the very best job they can. I believe they are committed to their jobs and passionately believe in the people's right to know. Many see their work as guarding the freedoms of their country and sense that it has significance well beyond just a transfer of information. Most of us would agree with that. Practically all of us are more thankful than we know for a free press. Yet that does not release any of us, media people included, from examining the nature of a reporting process that influences as well as reports. Though the media in general convey a certain non-Christian worldview in practically all of its efforts, we will confine our remarks to the journalistic efforts of television and the print media. There are at least four characteristics of American journalism that make its efforts dangerous, especially in reporting Christianity.

Media Journalism Is Powerful. So much has been said and read about the pervasiveness of television and other media. No extensive review is needed here. We know that 98 percent of American homes have at least one television, and that only sleep and work claim more of the average American's time than watching TV. We know that television's effects are especially powerful upon its viewers because of its ability to let the viewer see and experience (vicariously) its programming. Common sense and studies both tell us that we are imitative animals and we are impacted by what we watch. Newspapers, too, are pervasive. They are easily the most popular educational print materials sold. The most popular of the newspapers are, of course, not the ones bought for ideological reasons. The most popular are the general, major newspapers that offer a tie-in with our commercial culture and contain significant non-news drawing power. The selling points are coupons, entertainment features, and practical sections such as classified ads and local information. So newspapers, as well as television, give us a daily dose of a secular worldview. Radio and magazines are also a significant influence.

Their power comes not only from their pervasiveness, but also from their credibility. According to a recent Gallup poll, TV anchors Peter Jennings, Dan Rather, and Tom Brokaw are seen as believable by 90, 89, and 88 percent of the public, respectively, while the president scores only 68 percent. But the study cautions that "the news media sell believability foremost; presidents do not."[1] Part of that credibility must come from the fact that television is the majority's main window to the world. There is no basis for comparison. There are no other voices to help evaluate what is being reported and how it is being said. But regardless of the reason, credibility is both present and strong. Such credibility, though dwindling at the moment, has been long-lived. Not too many years ago television journalist Walter Cronkite was said to be the most trusted man in America. Credibility is power, the power to influence in everything said.

And certainly the celebrity status of many television journalists carries with it much power. Americans love celebrities. We make and follow them regularly, until their shooting stardom fizzles. For most celebrities, visibility is either irregular, short-lived, or both. Athletes have a few years in the spotlight. Movie stars may have more years, but their exposure is more sporadic. Politicians are less visible than most celebrities (except in an election year) and presidents, especially, are short-lived. Ronald Reagan has been the first president since Eisenhower (in the 1950s) and Nixon (in the early 1970s) to win two successive terms in office. Compare all of that type of celebrity status to a national news personality who is seen nightly for years on end and something becomes evident.

Newscasters like David Brinkley and the three mentioned above not only report the news, they *are* the news. Their opinions become important. We assume they would not be where they are if they did not know what they were talking about. People want to know what they think. After all, they are—ideally—above all the issues and have no special interests to promote.

The newscasters' power is exemplified in a conversation that took place between Senator Alan Cranston and journalist Dan Rather. During lunch a CBS aide approached Senator Cranston to say, "Senator, Mr. Rather will only have time for one more question."[2]

The arrogance that comes with such power is almost inevitable. Los Angeles *Times* bureau chief Jack Nelson, on comparing the press to the president of the United States, made this statement: "I don't see any reason why we shouldn't consider ourselves on equal footing with those we cover."[3] Where there is that kind of arrogance and power, the potential for destruction is great.

Media Journalism Is Prejudiced. There have been a number of recent studies dealing with objectivity in national media journalism. None have found objectivity. According to Gallup, close to half of the Americans surveyed "say the press is biased, with more perceiving a liberal rather than a conservative tilt. Yet people are more likely to blame shortcomings on commercial and interest group pressures rather than on journalists themselves."[4] A recent book would dispute that latter statement.

In a fascinating book entitled, *The Media Elite: America's New Powerbrokers*, a team of social scientists report on interviews with 238 journalists from newspapers, magazines, and TV news departments. The results point to prejudice, if one can assume that personal opinions affect the journalist's work. There is no basis for believing that journalists' perceptions of what is to be reported and how it is to be reported are any less affected by their personal views of reality than other persons'.

With that in mind let us explore some of the findings, limiting ourselves to those findings especially relevant to evangelical Christianity. The journalists surveyed categorized themselves as more liberal (54 percent) than conservative (17 percent) in number. Fifty percent checked "none" when it came to religion. Of those surveyed, only 8 percent attended church or synagogue weekly, and 86 percent said they seldom or never attend.[5] Compared with the population they serve (of whom never more than 22 percent have classified themselves as liberal, 40 percent attend church or synagogue weekly, and only 7 percent claim no religious affiliation) they definitely seem more liberal.[6] More specifically, journalists are more liberal on morality issues. Ninety percent of them believe women have the right to choose abortion, only 25 percent of them believe that homosexuality is wrong, and less than half agree with the Ten Commandments that adultery is wrong.[7] Most frightening of all, perhaps, are the findings concerning journalism students—the future of media reporting. They "take a quantum leap beyond their elders in criticizing America's economic and political institutions, while sharing their rejection of traditional social and cultural norms. They also profess admiration for liberal public figures and media organs, but disapprove of conservative newsmakers and news outlets."[8] It seems logical to assume that the leanings of journalists themselves invade their "objective reporting" and will continue to do so perhaps in a more pronounced way.

We see some news programs coming across as biased also. According to a study done by Michael Robinson and colleagues at George Washington University, news programs that can be seen as biased are biased in the liberal direction. For example, at NBC, of the percentage of news stories where bias could be detected, the "reports favored liberals over conservatives by better than a 4 to 1 margin."[9] And Robinson and crew did detect "bias by agenda" in CBS news coverage. "The network devoted 37 percent of its coverage to subjects perceived to reflect a liberal slant . . . 23 percent was devoted to subjects dear to conservative hearts."[10] Those statistics are not spectacular, and because they are not, the reality they point to may be more significant than we realize. It is the contention of this book that influence is more powerful and long-lasting when it is not blatant enough to cause a reaction. Such is the nature, and danger, of prejudicial reporting.

Media Journalism Is Hungry. It is extremely significant that American journalistic efforts are connected with commercial ventures. It is also significant that, especially on television, there is a certain amount of space that must be filled with "interesting and important" news.

Commercial ventures, news reporting included, are judged by more than one standard. But one standard is overwhelming enough to be the bottom line: how big an audience a program can attract. The bigger the audience, the more money the venture can make per effort. A few percentage points in the ratings or a slip in subscriptions can mean millions of dollars. It can also mean a search for new reporters. This all means that entertainment and drama enter into reporting. It also means that if no strongly interesting news is happening, some must be created. Daniel Boorstin noted this in his brilliant book, *The Image: A Guide to Pseudo-Events in America*. His belief is that our hunger for information, rather than truth as it is or is not, creates the market for made-up information. Michael O'Neill, a journalist for thirty years, agrees with him. He was quoted in an April 1986 issue of USA *Today* as saying, "The media are creating, shaping, and often distorting the informational base of decision making, magnifying as well as reporting the conflicts of power . . . life simply doesn't supply enough sensation to meet the media's daily needs." According to the article, an additional complication comes from the perceived need of the sensational. It is not the sensationalism that comes from depth of insight or thought. It emphasizes "action over thought, conflict over harmony, the exceptional over the normal, and negative over positive."

Media Journalism Is Combative. The press has approximately the same strategy as boxer Muhammad Ali. He revolutionized the boxing world by making "hype" as important as technical skills. He learned that audiences loved to hate an arrogant force. He learned that provoking people could force mistakes upon which he could capitalize. We (the audience) could never tell if he really meant the things he was saying about his opponents, or if we were just being used in a blatant ploy for our attention. Yes, Ali was, at his best, the best in the ring. He had the talent to back up the brazen manner. But the strategy not only advanced boxing styles and skills, it advanced showmanship.

The press is becoming known for its adversarial character. It is bordering on being a hostile witness, that is, having a point it would rather get across than limiting itself to the facts. "Yellow journalism" and the muckraking sensationalism of Teddy Roosevelt's day are making a comeback. The press seems ready to judge (negatively) everyone but itself. Abe Raskins, former *New York Times* editor, has said, "The press prides itself—as it should—on the vigor with which it excoriates malefactors in government, unions, and business, but its own inadequacies escape both its censure and its notice. . . . The real long-range menace to America's daily newspapers lies in the unshatterable smugness of their publishers and editors."[11] The same is true of television. Who decides maleficence? This "smug" crusade to find injustice or criminal activity is both popular and alarming. It can be valuable, but it is certainly dangerous. In cases like the Watergate scandal, many Americans felt the press was justified in its watchdog attitude. According to a Harris poll, 30 percent of Americans surveyed expressed a "great deal of confidence" in the press at that time. By 1981 that percentage had dropped to 16. We pay attention to the investigative reporting, but we are less and less confident of its objective accuracy.

Two cases in point that exemplify this type of journalism and our apprehension about it are the television show "60 Minutes" and the antics of Geraldo Rivera. The show "60 Minutes" has been at the top of the Nielsen ratings for years. In fact, it is one of the most popular television shows in history. Yet which of us would feel safe in getting a fair, unbiased interview if the "60 Minutes" correspondents knocked on our door? Most of us would assume their agenda would predestine the outcome and presentation of such an interview. Or perhaps we would consider Geraldo Rivera coming to our door. Here is a man who came into national prominence on the show "20/20." Almost weekly he would find someone or something to accuse. Perhaps some justice came from it. But the negative side of this kind of journalism was obvious in many of his investigative efforts. The empty sensationalism of such efforts was (un)graphically portrayed on national television when, after much promotional hype, the audience saw a gangster's vault containing nothing significant or even interesting. How symbolic. Even more illustrative of the danger of such investigative reporting is the case of Rivera being sued in a made-for-media police bust in which the allegations against the subjects were made before investigators found no evidence.

Geraldo is not the only one being sued. When General Westmoreland sued CBS for libel, or Israeli defense minister Ariel Sharon sued *Time* magazine, it was a sign of the times. People are defending themselves against perceived bias and the press is defending itself against perceived attacks of First Amendment rights. Indeed, there is combat happening and a combative mentality developing. Groups like Accuracy in Media are watchdogging the watchdogs (the press). Walter Cronkite accuses the Reagan administration of a "frontal attack" on the press. But he encourages the press to continue undaunted. In a USA *Today* article he concludes an exhortation to continue in "aggressive and fearless" reporting "if newspapers and broadcast stations are afraid . . . if they fear that the cost of courage to pursue their sacred obligation is too high—then what value is a First Amendment? What value is freedom unused?"[12] It sounds like an old Winston Churchill World War II speech, one that encourages soldiers in battle.

So we are in an environment where the press is defensive and offensive. The press is combative, partly because of its strategy and partly because of its reaction to decreased public allegiance. Some believe that the press has an agenda of its own, and that it is consciously trying to shape the American society. Such a view is expressed in Tim LaHaye's book, *The Hidden Censors*. Others believe that the press is not such a concentrated force for change as it is an extremely powerful filter through which only some things are allowed to pass, and most things are interpreted in the process. This view says the press may not have a unified purpose but does have a profound effect. *The Media Elite: America's New Powerbrokers* advocates this view. Newsman Robert McNeill said in *TV Guide* years ago, "Like the human digestive system, television alters what it consumes." For our purposes, it is not necessary to decide the exact agenda of the press in order to predict its effect if it becomes the reporter of evangelical Christianity.

Privacy and Piracy

Given the press's hunger for news and for leaning toward the provocative issues that increase ratings, the scrutiny of any major political office is a given. The scrutiny of the people who hold those offices, especially the presidency, entails analyzing everything they do and say or have done and said. Who can withstand such scrutiny? If we wonder why politicians' rhetoric is given to generalizations and platitudes, certainly one reason is that they know they will be held accountable for every detail and every innuendo of every detail. That is the life of a major politician. A recognized religious leader as president can expect no privacy, especially not the privacy of his religious practice. His prayer closet will be bugged, his almsgiving will be questioned. If his left hand doesn't know what his right hand is doing (Matt. 6:3), he can read about it in the newspaper. And he can be almost certain it will be interpreted in a negative way. Given the previously mentioned propensity of the press for the negative over the positive and conflict over peace, his every move will be nailed with a "cruci-fiction" of interpretation. When Pat Robertson first declared his candidacy, UPI ran a story about people who question his charitable giving as politically motivated. "Doonesbury" cartoons had him caricatured as speaking in tongues at a press conference. The caricaturing of presidents or candidates is a time-honored tradition. Christians must wonder, though, if the caricaturing of aspects of Christianity is what God would want. The Scripture is clear about providing a clear witness. It warns us about the inevitability of mockers (2 Pet. 3:3), but it warns us too that we should resist public practices that can be a stumbling block for fledgling believers (Rom. 14:14-21; 1 Cor. 8:9). My question is, how can any religious leader as president avoid the publicity that caricatures his religion and thus avoid becoming a stumbling block for immature believers? How much more will be lost than gained for the kingdom?

"If This Is Christian Politics, Forget It"

Any evangelical celebrity as president, or as holder of any high-visibility office, will have his every act or policy decision linked to his Christianity. A discerning evangelical celebrity as president would have to make a distinction between his own opinions and the Lord's direct command, as Paul did in 1 Corinthians 7:25. Yet neither the press nor the public would be so discerning. Each act of a so obvious representative of Christianity would be a reflection on God in the undiscerning mind. The evangelical celebrity as president would be put in a position where his religion would be interpreted through his policy. Evangelism would have a major new handicap to overcome. Every mistake in office would be viewed as a product of and witness to the ineffectiveness of Christianity. Every slipup of normal knowledge will be taken as a mark against revealed knowledge. The comments would couple human mistakes with God's inerrancy. "If that is Christian politics, I don't want any part of Christianity." "If God directed the selecting of that guy for a cabinet member, I'm not sure I want Him guiding my life." It would be like the car I spotted while at a stoplight one day. As I looked in the opposite lane across the red light, I saw a car that looked as if it had gone through a demolition derby. The side was bashed in, the front grill was crushed, and the windshield was cracked. In the front license plate holder sat a plate that read, "God Is My Co-pilot." Failure to disconnect God from our own mistakes can really get in the way of our witness. I doubt that a religious celebrity as president could ever make that disconnection in the minds of the public.

Matthew 6:22-23 quotes Jesus, "The lamp of the body is the eye; if therefore your eye is clear, your whole body will be full of light. But if your eye is bad, your whole body will be full of darkness. If therefore the light that is in you is darkness, how great is the darkness!"

The election of a religious celebrity to any prominent political office, especially that of president, puts not only the person but the religion in the public eye. What is the eye of the public? Right now, it is the national media. Some explanation of the above Scripture will let us see what will happen if a major part of the secular press's agenda is the analysis and interpretation of evangelical Christianity.

The passage uses two adjectives to describe the "eye," that is, the mean through which we perceive truth. The original Greek for "clear" is *haplous*. In other passages in Scripture the word is used for "generous." In 2 Corinthians 9:13, Romans 12:8, and James 1:5, the word is used in the sense of giving liberally. The word implies that there is a desire to be generous and to see the other person at his best. On the other hand, the Greek word for "bad" in this passage is *poneros* (also translated the "evil eye"). The word is used in other Scriptures to mean grudging, stingy—like the testimony of a hostile witness. Deuteronomy 15:9 cautions people not to have a base thought in their heart against being generous. It is an evil eye that sees how much it can get out of something and how little it can give. So then, one eye is generous and one is grudging. Which would you see the national media as being?

In fact, the eye that can only look at a part of something to analyze it will miss its entire truth. The gospel reported by the press, or the actions of Christian celebrities, would be given the evil eye. The gospel would be overexposed, oversimplified, overanalyzed, and overlooked. Perhaps the press would not intend maliciousness, but the very nature of its reporting would cause misunderstanding.

The gospel was not designed to be dumped upon unprepared people. The Scripture says that Christ came when the right time had come (Gal. 4:4). The implication is that there must be a readiness to receive the gospel. When there is no readiness the gospel can be rejected, not because of its content, but because of its timing. It is a principle in physics, and in faith, that for every action there is a reaction. If the nation were presented with evangelical Christianity night after night as a part of the news, chances are there would be a negative reaction in many lives. Who can know when is the right time for such a presentation? The local pastor who knows his people can know. The Christian who is sensitive to a friend's spiritual journey can know. And certainly the Holy Spirit who leads someone to listen to Christian television or radio at the right time knows. But the national media does not know or care about timing of the gospel presentation.

The gospel would be oversimplified. There are certain basic beliefs in Christianity that must be agreed upon before any single issue in Christianity can be fully comprehended. For example, how can the public comprehend our evangelical pro-life stance without the basic knowledge that we believe God knit us together in the womb (Isa. 44:2, 24) or that we believe God has a purpose for every life (Eph. 2:10)? Without that basic understanding, the evangelical pro-life stance looks like cold moralistic condemnation. If the stance is presented without explanation of the prerequisite belief, many issues will bring oversimplification without understanding.

Evangelical Christians have the knowledge and the sympathy to present the entire context of the stance. The media has neither the revealed knowledge nor the natural sympathy to present the entire context of the stance. In fact, it is a paradox that even though the media is hungry for issues, it lives on a no-depth diet. The media in general, television in particular, present the information in brief and simplistic segments. The time crunch prevents a full view of any issue. And what is left, for the supposed lowest-common-denominator audience with its short attention span, is a momentary and fleeting glimpse at issues of depth and complexity. The hungry press chews up and spits out lots of material in a limited time and space, insuring that people will not digest such subtleties as our unique perspective or our scriptural guidelines. That kind of simplicity we would do well to avoid.

The gospel would be overanalyzed. The press operates with scientific methodology. This methodology involves subjecting any entity to dissection into its constituent elements. But spirituality cannot be fully understood using scientific methodology. In fact, that process taken alone will insure misunderstanding of Christianity.

The method of scientific inquiry is valid for some matters. In mechanical or structural inquiry the scientific method is of great value. When parts of the whole can be examined separately and in minute detail, one can reconstruct a better machine. Cancer may someday be cured by cellular examination and manipulation. Computers will become even more efficient by technology's fascination with minutiae. Some outstanding news stories will be written by some reporter's digging for details. But when it comes to the spiritual life or even personal relationships, breaking things down into details reaches a point of diminishing returns. Things are not always easier to take in bits. Philosopher Thomas Hobbes described it well: "For it is with the mysteries of our religion as with wholesome pills for the sick, which swallowed whole have the virtue to cure, but chewed are for the most part cast up again without effect."[13] Overanalysis occurs when a narrow method of investigation is applied to a phenomenon that is beyond reason and closer to passion. Romance can be investigated by dissection and reason, but it cannot be fully understood or experienced in that process. Humor can be analyzed in like manner—and lost in the process. Intuition, trust, and hope may all be studied, but none will be completely grasped by rational analysis. They are of a different nature. And any one of them, when studied extensively, will dissipate by that study. The French thinker Pascal was right when he said, "The heart has its reasons which the reason does not understand." Pascal the scientist knew that not everything could be studied effectively with the scientific method.

Evangelicals are not against reasoned investigation. Nothing in a valid faith will contradict reason. God gave us minds that can grasp both faith and scientific fact. But the secular world has not come to grips with the limitations of reason. It is fanatical in its use of reason, just as some religious groups are fanatical in their use of faith. We simply want to recognize that the form of scientific reasoning called media analysis, when squinting to see religion, will fail to grasp and communicate the whole truth. Like the story of the three blind men examining an elephant for the first time, each will define Christianity only in terms of the part presently in its limited grasp. They may describe that part in great detail, but if they do not participate with a generous eye, taking in the whole picture, the image they convey will be much distorted. The consequences for evangelism could be disastrous. If that image is the only one nonbelievers are receiving because of their dependence on the media as their eye to the world, how great will be the darkness!

Notes

1. Who Likes the Press—And Who Doesn't," U.S. *News & World Report,* 27 January 1986, 78.
2. S. Robert Lichter, Stanley Rothman, and Linda S. Lichter, *The Media Elite: America's New Powerbrokers* (Bethesda, Md.: Adler & Adler, 1986), 27.
3. John R. Burke, "Five Votes Shy of a Load," *Vital Speeches of the Day,* 13 July 1985, 7.

4. "Who Likes the Press," 78.
5. Ibid., 21.
6. Ibid., 29.
7. Gallup Poll/Princeton Religion Research Center, "Scholastic Update," 1 March 1985.
8. Lichter, Rothman, Lichter, 294.
9. *Psychology Today*, July 1985, 16.
10. Ibid.
11. Burke, 701.
12. USA *Today Magazine*, September 1986, 34.
13. Thomas Hobbes, *Leviathan* (New York: Washington Square Press, 1964), 268.

FIVE

"The Problem with Every Government": Sin

I believe in political equality. But there are two opposite reasons for being a democrat. You may think all men so good that they deserve a share in the government of the commonwealth, and so wise that the commonwealth needs their advice. . . . On the other hand, you may believe fallen men to be so wicked that not one of them can be trusted with any irresponsible power over his fellows. That I believe to be the true ground of democracy.

C. S. *Lewis*

Something in us will not let any of us govern very well. The problem lies not in our methods or systems, but in our hearts. The problem is the very first issue addressed in Scripture after creation. According to the Bible, our problem with governing stems from our resistance to being governed. We have always liked the idea that we could, by some special knowledge or some better device, have a better system than the one presently in place.

Adam and Eve, our parents and prototypes, are pictured trying to extend their power. The thought that new knowledge would automatically make things better has always been enticing. Our first parents believed that new knowledge would add a capacity of power. So, thinking with their desires, they reached beyond God's first plan for their lives (Gen. 3:11). Going beyond their specific limits, however, they lost more than they gained. They lost the direct fellowship with God that came with doing His work His way, and the work itself became much more difficult to accomplish (Gen. 3:17-19).

That ambition and rebellion had an irreversible effect on our nature. Our tendency is still to reach for power. Since all life is power, the reasonable assumption is that the Christian community should have their share. It is an illusion, though, to believe that governmental power is better because a believer holds it. History shows no such correlation. The record is both sad and humorous. The Hebrews thought that if God's man would just rule them, certainly they would be governed perfectly. But the record of their kings is atrocious. Their priests and prophets were God's gifts to balance sinful leadership. Centuries later, when Emperor Constantine was converted, many believed that there would not only be relief from persecution but righteousness in office. Yet the records show injustice toward nonbelievers and questionable actions in spite of Constantine's conversion. His successors in Christian political leadership could be seen as a comedy of heirs. Actually, no signs of perfection appeared for the first five hundred years after Constantine; then things got worse. Few medieval kings were any more inspiring because they governed as Christians in supposedly Christian nations. A few saintly ones, like French crusader King Louis IX (1214–1270) were renowned for heading righteous governments, but men like Louis were exceptional. Even after the great theologian Thomas Aquinas had put forward the concept that God had delegated spiritual power to kings, Christian kings like Philip IV (1268–1314) of France used the theory to exalt secular power over ecclesiastical power. Talk about biting the hand that feeds you!

Since those years, much serious thought has been devoted to explaining the nature of God's involvement in governing the state. The political theorists began with definitions of the state that range from "it is a direct creation of God" to "it is a simple social contract postulated by man as social animal." Yet no theory about the nature of the state, or what God's involvement in government should be, has changed the world's record of flawed government. No Christian leader, however dedicated to the faith, has been the solution to flawed government. Both theory and leader are devices, mechanical answers to a deeper problem of avoiding God's direct government.

It is tempting to swallow the notion that we are becoming unflawed as a governed people with time and learning. Two American reformers earlier this century did much to popularize this belief. They were more optimistic about man's ability to progressively approach perfection with government. Both a Christian and a humanist voiced very attractive hopes. After World War I, pastor Walter Rauschenbusch became a most eloquent spokesman for the Social Gospel. He identified the phrase "Thy kingdom come, Thy will be done on earth as it is in heaven" as a command of God for this present age. He believed he saw a "growing perfection," and his followers were even more optimistic than he about "Christianizing the entire social order."[1] The democratic ideal was being provided a religious sanction; the perennial civil religion was blooming again. (It is interesting that many religious conservatives today echo some of the ideals of these liberals gone by.) The mistake was, of course, that the social gospelers underestimated the enormity of sin. They believed "love covers a multitude of sins." It does. But sin infests the entire multitude of lovers. The Social Gospel movement could only see the difference between good and evil, not fix it.

Educator John Dewey believed man's problem was not sin, but ignorance. Man simply did not know his potential, said Dewey. As soon as he could investigate by experiment, whether in education or science or government, he would learn his way out of his problems. If people were repeatedly offered the way of love and justice and equality, of course they would happily take it. Selfishness and greed would fade away. Man would find his way up, head first. Yet it should be evident by now that thinking better cannot be equated with being better.

The return to reality began with theologian Reinhold Niebuhr, who understood the true nature of man. Niebuhr stated plainly that shallow sentimental optimism was worse than useless. To recognize the "essential goodness of men without realizing how evil good men can be" was a monumental mistake, he said. His book *Moral Man and Immoral Society*, though it tends to equate morality with religion, still stands as an important rejection of politics that assume love and reason transcend sin. He recognized that we use evil to hold evil in check and that political answers could only approximate God's will in this life. He knew that power was a necessity for political action, but that there was no "ethical force strong enough to place inner checks upon the use of power if its quantity is inordinate." Therefore we dare not trust in a man's goodness, but we must react to his specific political plans. He noted America's tendency to choose "a messiah rather than a political leader committed to a specific political program."[2] Finally, he was most valuable in pointing out that, while there are absolutes in faith, the mistake of political religion is to absolutize what is relative in politics. He claimed that religion can be a great source of confusion in politics because of its tendency to take a stand as leader where it should be playing the role of prophet. Prophets were not political leaders. They questioned and corrected and influenced political leaders.[3] Niebuhr understood not only human sin but the need for prophecy in all ages.

The Sin That Limits Us

Adam and Eve's choice was not between being limited and unlimited. Their choice was to be limited by obedience to God or limited by internal evil. In their quest for wisdom and control, they had missed a most important consideration: we cannot use something without internalizing all aspects of that thing and being limited by it. The act of swallowing the "forbidden fruit" was more than literal. It meant that the evil as well as the good they reached for became a part of them. They sought to have a "knowledge of good and evil." They may have assumed that they could control it, that they could keep it at arm's length. But knowledge in the Bible and in life is relationship. When Scripture says, "Adam knew Eve, his wife, and she conceived, and bare Cain" (Gen. 4:1, KJV), the "knowing" is not mental objectivity, but intimate relationship. Just as Adam and Eve became a part of one another, so it is with our knowledge of anything. It becomes a part of us; not only its good but its evil side are ingested in its entirety.

Science has recognized this truth. It has been the assumption of psychotherapy that simply teaching new information will not cure crippling mental problems. Our previously swallowed assumptions need to be brought out, pointed out, thought out, kicked out, and replaced. During the course of many brain surgery procedures, Dr. Wilder Penfield was able to demonstrate that memories are not just stored objective information. They are experiences that lie dormant in their entirety. In these surgeries, in which the patients remained awake, Dr. Penfield's electric probe stimulated the brain cells that recalled events. The events were not just remembered, they were relived. The patients could smell the same smells, hear the same music, experience the same emotions as in the original event.[4] The original event had affected the patient long after the patient had experienced the event. So we are made in such a way that what we use or grasp changes us and lives inside of us.

Happily Ever After Each Other

We have already discussed (in Chapter One) the different natures of church and state, or more accurately, Christianity and civil government. Christianity is strongest when its only force is persuasion; civil government's ultimate strength is its ability to use force. Christianity was made to expand; civil government has definite weaknesses in its expansion. Christianity has its authority from above; our civil government has its authority by the consent of the governed. Such are differences in their natures at present. A further question to be considered now is: how could their combining change their natures for the future? If evangelicals reach for the political fruit as a tool for increasing their influence, we will pay a price higher than we realize. There is a familiar saying between lovers: "I love you not only for what you are, but for what I become when I am with you." It is an affirmation that we are profoundly changed in intimate relationship. Our consumer mentality that suggests that we can use and dispose of anything without being affected does not take into account the fact that we are being constantly changed. Because of that fact, memorialized by Adam and Eve and some forbidden fruit, we must watch closely what we grasp so that we can protect our nature from further confusion. That is as true for institutions as it is for individuals.

The most dangerous quality of politics is the thirst for power. The difference between Christianity that operates in politics because of its civil responsibility and Christianity that longs for political power is quantum. Robert Dahl has written a book, *Who Governs?* in which he contrasts *homo civicus* and *homo politicus*—civic man and political man. He basically writes that civic man is a social being. He knows the quality of his life depends upon the health of the society in which he lives. He improves the environment for relationships by his activities in society, including his vote. He does not put the importance of government above duties family, church, and friends unless the government threatens to limit freedoms he sees as important.

Political man, on the other hand, regards political involvement as a way of gratifying his needs and getting his way. He is much more in love with power than civic man. He attempts to gain control over civil man, and only when civil man perceives that threat will he take action to thwart political man. For political man, politics is a way of life, and power is the breakfast of champions. For civic man, relationships are a way of life, while politics and power are only periodic necessities.

If Christians strive to be true to the New Testament, they would be highly suspicious of political man. Nowhere in the New Testament does it exhort individuals to political leadership. But political, power relationships are forbidden by

Christ or transformed into an act of service (Matt. 20:25-28). Christendom must not ingest politics in general, or its focus and character will change drastically. Cooperation is appropriate, continuing conversation is a mutual duty at all times, but marriage is out.

The wisdom of a fourth-grader will close the point. When the class was asked by the teacher to do some creative writing, they took out their paper. "Write a story of romance," said the teacher. Johnny was finished within a few moments. His story had three sentences:

He said, "Will you marry me?"
She said, "No."
And they lived happily ever after.

Killer Tendencies

Evangelicals have stayed away from politics for good reason. Pastors have avoided discussions about politics in the local church for good reason. Many of our parents taught us that conversations about politics (and religion) could be hazardous to the health of relationships, and they had good reason. Part of politics is the art of gaining control. It is a manifestation of our sinful nature that can cause every deliberation over power to become a power struggle itself. Experience has taught us and intuition warns us that politics is volatile. It can change in an instant from helpful to hurtful, from service-oriented to dominating, from benign to malignant and back again. Politics is not just a subject, it is a positioning. The very topic has a subtle way of calling us from trust to suspicion. Even conversations that end amicably leave lingering distances if the conversants are not in perfect agreement. The ideal of pluralism—an ideal that we insist is what makes America free—becomes more frustration than goal in political conversation. The ideal of pluralism that should safeguard our relationships by not insisting on agreement before togetherness belongs to a realm of maturity that many admire but few desire. In fact, there is something hidden in opinions thrown out, like a stone in a snowball, that changes conversations to war rather than fun competition. If we could isolate and extract that thing, we might go far in keeping people from becoming enemies.

American politics will continue to be a competition between interest groups and individuals. There are only two scenarios in which that norm would change: either we would have switched to an alien form of government, or the Lord would have come again. Otherwise, we will live with a system of government in which the pursuit of national interests entails the profit of some special interest groups at the expense of others. The danger to our peace is the amount of profit and loss. The smaller the gain of one group over the other, the more equity we have in our nation. Equity both promotes and controls competition. Gross inequity almost insures rebellion and fanaticism. But a system in which both sides of any issue have much more to lose than that particular battle, and in which the loss of that battle will not mortally wound their cause, can thrive on competition. Each side can be kept stimulated and more attentive because of the close competition. Each side can build a life that does not depend upon, and will not be destroyed by, the outcome of the competition. Such is the ideal for which the framers of our Constitution strove. Creating a series of checks and balances that would insure as little inequity as possible and make tyranny by any group unlikely, they gave us all a great gift. But the stone in the snowball could still ruin it. Even great and mighty giants can be felled with a stone. What is the stone hidden in other forms? And once we find it, can we extract it? And if we can extract it, will we?

The Central Problem in Individuals

The stone in the snowball is ego; ego always wants to be at the center of things. This does not sound like a surprising or difficult concept to grasp. In fact, it is so familiar that it goes without heed. It is not spiritual enough for evangelicals to address; it is not unusual enough for others to notice. Yet ego is at the heart of the matter. Let us first define the concept of ego as it is used here, then go on to explore its destructive capabilities.

In a way, I dislike depending on a Freudian term to define so important a problem. As an evangelical I have this feeling that I should be able to come up with some strictly biblical term that would solve such a world problem. But the very fact that I desire to twist understanding and control terms to make me and my group look good is evidence of the problem itself: ego. Samuel Taylor Coleridge once said, "He who begins by loving Christianity better than truth will proceed by loving his own sect or church better than Christianity, and end in loving himself better than all." No, while I do take comfort in knowing that the Bible's descriptions of people match and predate the term *ego*, it is still the secular term that is helpful in analyzing the problem. We need not go too deeply into psychoanalytic theory. To do so would cloud the concept. The common understanding of the term is valuable: the Ego (which I will henceforth spell with a capital *E*) is the "I" of everything. I will use capital *E* in Ego to connote the narcissistic emphasis. The Ego projects itself into the middle of every issue. The Ego determines the interest in, and understanding of, any issue. The Ego is active in protecting the individual's identity from confusion and intrusion. The Ego is not synonymous with sin; sin is more subtle and negative. The Ego is not evil. All of the above functions are necessary to a healthy personality. Relationships are built on the presupposition of individual identity, and sickness inhabits relationships when any of the individuals' identities are confused or diminished. A sense of relevancy is built on the relationship of an issue to an individual's identity. Again, the relationship is unhealthy when the identity is tied too closely to the issue so that either issue or identity is less than distinct. The Ego, then, is not a problem. The size of the Ego, or its proportion to the whole, can be a problem. A piece of gravel in a snowball is insignificant; a rock makes the snowball a weapon.

Destruction is inherent in political strategy when Ego concerns are the motivation for the effort. The Ego concerns are, in our popular nonclinical definition, the driving force to make ourselves the center of every effort and the standard of measure for every policy. Ego is the leaven that turns our gratitude for privileges into an arrogant attitude of privilege, then into an assumption that being privileged is a right. Such a transformation is recorded many times in the New Testament; it is microcosmed in Luke 18:9-14. The Pharisee is privileged with the spiritual leadership of the times, but he lets that privilege turn to arrogance. Foremost in his mind is that he ranks better than others. "I thank you that I am not like other men." His position has become in his mind such a fixed right that it does not occur to him to ask for forgiveness or correction. It is the habit of those who are privileged to turn privilege from a responsibility into a protected ranking. And it is easier for us to protect our ranking by institutionalizing it, rather than by continuing the effort that led to it. This desire to make "I" the higher standard of measure is the beginning of sin (Gen. 3:5).

Self-righteousness can be institutionalized. The first institutionalizing of self-righteousness can happen within a recognized church structure. For example, ordination, meant to be a recognition of God's particular call, can become itself substitution for a person's direct dependence on God. A pastor or bishop may lose all humility and exercise his authority without any regard for the Lord of the church. The second institutionalizing of self-righteousness can occur in the political sphere. For example, a voter can intend for his religious leader's attainment of office to be a mandate for his religion to be the norm. It is this sin that we must keep separate from state. It provides the believer with a false source of security; it infects the state with a skewed sense of sovereignty. No institution can perpetuate individual righteousness, at least not from an evangelical point of view.

The Central Problem in Groups

Such Ego tendencies are every bit as characteristic of groups as they are of individuals. We would do well to recognize that we are social beings who not only magnify our individual tendencies by group but intensify our individual evil possibilities in groups. The importance of group life is documented both in Scripture and in simple sociological observation. Since God determined that it is "not good for man to be alone" (Gen. 2:18), the effects others have on us and how we sin have been recorded. The influence of group dynamics in shaping the perceptions and actions of its constituent individuals is evident. Also, the personalities of groups themselves are important to note. Let us take a moment to explore them both.

Our individual Ego concerns lead us to be a part of a group. Different kinds of groups influence our interaction with the world. But they do not necessarily diminish our Ego tendencies toward being the center of attention and the standard of measure. These groups can be found described in many contemporary sociology textbooks.

One group is the *primary group*, a supreme example of which is the family. The primary group pays intense attention to us (many times reinforcing our "center of things" perspective). It molds our values and our method of operation. It is the significant source of fact and interpretation of reality. It can give us stability and security and a sense of belonging while we deal with our environment. It can also be instrumental in determining who leads what groups (see Gen. 27). But the primary group is not our primary concern here. Though analysis of our primary groups can give us insights into our previous development and one's contemporary close relationships, our interest here is rather in the groups chosen as resources for societal influence. Those groups reflect our concerns, and we use them as devices to manipulate our environment.

Most larger groups to which we turn are of our own choosing, reflecting our own purposes. They are called *secondary groups*. Their influence upon us may not be as personal as the primary group's. Our influence upon them is not as direct or significant. Yet we see them as our chance for our greatest societal impact. The contrast between primary and secondary groups become evident by examples. While a discipleship group may be an example of a primary group, the entire church or universal church is an example of a secondary group. A few close cronies who discuss politics make up a primary group; a political party is an example of a secondary group. Longtime neighbors who wish to protect each other from harm comprise a primary group; the armed forces are a secondary group. When we become a part of a secondary group, a plus outweighs the minus in regards to Ego gratification. The minus is, of course, that our ability to impact the course of such a group is reduced proportionately to the number of other constituents with our status. This frustrates some idealists, who do not realize how little they will be able to impact a large group. Such people can become disillusioned as that realization confronts them. Yet the benefits of belonging to such a large group are significant, especially in relation to one's Ego concerns. Two such benefits that feed and nurse our Ego concerns should be noted.

First, belonging to a secondary group gives an individual a sense that his deeds have a broader impact, a more profound effect. One may convince his cronies that a certain public policy is unwise, but if he can be a part of a group that actually effects the change of that public policy, he has some "bragging rights." An individual may not need to be the center of a group if that group is at the center of things that matter. He can borrow enough of the group's importance to gratify his Ego concerns. This benefit of belonging to a secondary group is so strong that it makes individuals willing to die for such a group cause. Those slain in civil rights causes, those slain in each war, those who endanger their lives daily for people or ideals rather than profit, testify to our desire to have an impact in this world.

Second, the larger secondary group has the power and importance to dispense a special recognition to the individual that a primary group does not have. Our Ego needs may be satisfied by identification with a group's impact, but how much more rewarding it is if that group actually recognizes our value as individuals. There are times when we sense that primary groups must confirm our significance out of their own survival needs, or because it is their job. Parents may tell their son he is great because they want him to be great or because he could never be anything but great in their eyes. The son's Ego needs are addressed positively in that recognition but not satisfied objectively. If, however, a large group gives him a bar on his shoulder, or a title in his precinct, then there is new potence in the recognition of his value. For most individuals, the size and increased objectivity of the group does much to answer but not moderate one's Ego needs.

The result of the investment in the group, then, is a magnified reliance upon the group's importance to the constituent's Ego concerns. Also, the group has an Ego accumulated from its constituents. The group needs to be the center; the group needs to be the standard of measure. Furthermore, every group has two personalities. One relates to the world. Its objectives in relation to the world are usually published. That agenda is the personality (*persona* literally means "mask") by which others come to recognize its overt goals. In a large secondary group this outside agenda personality is usually written in clearly stated goals. In a church it is the statement of beliefs and/or a mission statement. One may, after reading such a statement, be able to differentiate this local church from another local church or this denomination from that denomination. No such statement has been written for all Christendom except the Bible. In a political party the objective goal statement usually can be found in the updated party platform. The voters are to compare the platforms of two (or more) parties. The group also has an inward agenda, one concerned with itself. There is an investment of individual selves that makes the secondary group grow more responsive to its constituency than to the agenda outside its constituency. That's the other personality of group life. The group becomes an entity that not only has an impact on behalf of its constituents but turns its agenda toward its constituents. It becomes a means of increasing their privilege as well as a tool for their service. It becomes a mirror as well as a window, but many times it does not realize it!

The subtle effect of Ego upon a group is that the group projects its needs and values upon all mankind. The group turns to the world for answers to the group's needs. This tendency is even more pronounced with increased dominion. It makes the group both arrogant and ignorant when it comes to using power. Niebuhr describes this phenomenon:

> The moral attitudes of dominant and privileged groups are characterized by universal self-deception and hypocrisy. The unconscious and conscious identification of their special interests with general interests and universal values . . . is equally obvious in the attitude of classes. The reason why privileged classes are more hypocritical than underprivileged ones is that special privilege can be defended . . . only by proving that it contributes something to the good of the whole. Since inequalities are greater than could possibly be defended rationally, the intelligence of privileged groups is usually applied to the task of inventing specious proofs for the theory that universal values spring from, and that general interests are served by, *the special privileges which they hold.*[5] [emphasis mine]

Notice that it is not the group's truth that is being defended, but the group's privilege or position. That is not a matter of truth; that is a matter of Ego.

When the focus of a group is upon self, the inevitable conflict with other "self groups" produces less than moral behavior (as well as less than moral rationalization). Dr. M. Scott Peck, in analyzing the subject of group evil at the My Lai massacre, shares this observation: "For many years it has seemed to me that human groups tend to behave in much the same ways as human individuals—except at a level that is more primitive and immature than one might expect. Why this is so—why the behavior of groups is strikingly immature—why they are, from a psychological standpoint, less than the sum of their parts—is a question beyond my capacity to answer."[6] When we speak of the degeneration of group Ego into group evil, we are speaking of a process in which the evil is *not* inevitable. Nazi government in Germany began as a source of pride for the German people after their defeat in World War I. It restored to them the esteem that comes with group Ego. But in the conflict of World War II, the extermination of 6 million Jews was a result of Ego rationalization turned into evil destruction. Again, the agenda was not that of finding the truth, but that of striving for position. Even the *threat* of conflict to a power group can provoke its Ego to evil destruction. When the religious cult following Jim Jones had withdrawn from the world to set up its own little kingdom in Guyana, a congressman visited—for the purpose of inspection only. There was no action being taken yet by the United States government, but the congressman's mere presence ignited an ambush and a mass suicide of more than nine hundred people. Clearly, not philosophy but position was being defended. History gives us other examples of more passive, subtle forms of evil that spring from defending the position of a group during conflict. The 1986 movie *The Mission* depicts one such historical example. Jesuit priests create a mission in South America with the jungle Indians. They live with, love, and teach the Indians about God under the Roman Catholic church's protective custody, which shields the Indians from being material in governments' slave trade. When Spain and Portugal threaten the privileged status of the Roman Catholic church, it, in turn, pressures the Jesuits to withhold further protection of the Indians. The political realities produce obvious self-centered results. Again, political conflict that threatens the group's position produces behavior opposite from the group's ideal. One is tempted to explain it away in the words of one of the movie's characters, "Thus is the world." But the church representative counters with an admission of personal responsibility (the only antidote to group evil): "Thus have we made the world. Thus have I made it."

A Delicate Surgery

Once we have noted the norm of Ego and the resulting self-centeredness, the question arises whether it is possible to separate personal investment in a group from selfish ambition of a group. In that process of growth from healthy involvement to malignant dominion, there must be some treatment, perhaps an extraction, that can prevent self-destruction by group aggrandizement. There is such a treatment. It involves early detection, relentless limitation, and radiating faith.

It is difficult to determine when a healthy view of oneself as a worthy person (that is God's view—Psalm 8), or an accurate appraisal of one's group as valuable, turns into "centeredness." It is difficult because the signs of worth and pride are often the same. For example, in our city many cars wear the virtues of the church named, "______: the church that cares." Some churches offer a more perfect example of the point: a pun. One reads, "Life begins at Calvary." Calvary is, of course, not only the place of the cross but the name of the church. Another church, whose name includes the word *First* because of chronological foundation, advertises their congregation as "The First Family." It could be that all of these churches are simply and sincerely doing the best they know to invite folks to their church so that the folks can meet the Lord. But any church can easily slip into self-centeredness, where wearing the bumper sticker is a source of pride and positioning. (I have never seen a bumper sticker that said humbly, "______: just one of God's churches.") In any institution it is difficult to tell where reasonable self-esteem turns into self-centeredness and self-centeredness turns into idolatry. But that does not mean we should not try to detect such a transformation. Probably the best scriptural instrument for differentiating healthy self-esteem from self-centeredness is found in 1 Corinthians 13:4-7. Genuine love is the antithesis of self-centeredness. If the qualities of love that are listed could be used as a checklist of attitudes, perhaps the transformation of Ego could be detected. When asked in the form of questions applied to opposing people or groups, the qualities provide a high standard of insight. Am I patient with them? Am I kind when I talk of them? Do I envy them? Do I vaunt myself (or my group or my cause) over them instead of uplifting them as people? Am I seeking them or desiring to see myself in them? Original sin begins again every time our own power becomes our focus and our own increase is a delight to our eyes. Original sin proceeds every time we accept a voice that confirms that focus. Our group can easily supplant the serpent.

In this context the phrase "relentless limitation" refers to purity of motive. The words of Colossians 3:23 are as true in our participation in the political realm as in anything else, "Whatever you do, do your work heartily, as for the Lord rather than for men." It is, indeed, tempting to work for men—ourselves, or our group—rather than for the Lord. The relentless limitation that is so necessary is limitation on our imperialism—the spread of ourselves as the center of things. As individuals or as groups, our constant temptation is to swallow up others rather than serve them. We want to make them a part of our agenda rather than offer to become a part of their lives. We want to help by conquering. When Christ spoke to his disciples about greatness (Matt. 20:20-28; Mark 9:33-35; Luke 22:24-27), he did not censure their desire for influence, but he limited their attitude of imperialism. They were not to "lord over" people, they were to be at people's service, as he had been.

How can we, as groups or individuals, limit ourselves in intention but not activity? Consistent spiritual self-examination can alert us to a spreading disease. Some commonsense questions will help. What do we know of the people we intend to serve, especially the opposition, from their own mouths? How closely do we relate to them? How can we be there "incarnate" to walk among them? What can they teach us? When Peter tells Christians to "honor all men" (1 Pet. 2:17), he is limiting our approach to people; he is de-arrogating us! That is a relentless necessity.

We in America are fortunate to have a system of government that, in its present form, is almost impervious to major perversion. We can speak our opinions without moderation and have the system act as the balancing force. The consequences for nonmoderation, it should be noted, are relational separation. But, as far as the system goes, there is good reason to have confidence that little real harm will come to our neighbor because of our political extremes. Yet our faith must not be in our system of government ("Do not trust in princes, in mortal man, in whom there is no salvation" Ps. 146:3). Our characters are not transformed, our hearts are not sensitized, nor are our minds led into more truth by government. Only by placing our confidence in God's sovereignty are we able to relinquish our private imperialism "for the country's good." No turn of political fortune will frustrate his final purpose. Political absolutism in the name of God can be a distrust of God—a coup d'etat of His sovereignty. Does that mean we do not work politically for those policies and candidates in which we believe? Of course not. My friend Marv Rooks says that we in this country are waiting for Christ's return; we have the choice to wait in an outhouse or a living room. But while we care and work, we do not care *too* much. We do not place our reliance upon legislative conquests that control people but do not change them. Faith in God is both the motivation for—and the limitation of—our work.

Separation of Sin and State

If the Ego is the tendency toward self-centered immaturity, the last step of Ego unchecked is an effort toward dominance. The desire of the Ego is not for cooperation (which is complicated, and which requires time and effort), but for control over our lives *and* over others' lives. Furthermore, when Ego is transformed from an immature self-centeredness into an active effort to dominate others, our next step is to reach for devices that will allow us to dominate. The most overt device of dominance is political power: the state. How we relate to the state will determine whether we are using it as an expression of our individuality, as a platform for our own self-centeredness, or as a weapon for our dominance. Separation of self and state is not possible, nor is separation of sinner and state. But as believers we must separate ourselves from the use of the state for dominance. How can we relate to political power in a way that will allow us to express our individuality without giving into the sin of attempted political domination?

Evangelical Christians have a chance to model self-imposed limitations. Ideological combat in this world is seldom possible (or wise) to avoid. Christians have a distinct worldview that has its basis in a purpose beyond this world. The people in the world and of the world will not agree on this basis, so there will be conflict (John 16:33). The conflict is legitimate. In a world where people search for meaning, and answers to that search are so different, disagreements are inevitable. The conflicts, though, can be opportunities to witness. They are also our opportunities to model restraint in the use of power.

Christians in ideological conflict with the world can model what the world has not often seen—persons placing a limit on how much power they will stockpile. The world needs this kind of witness, for war is not what it used to be. Combat once meant killing individuals. Now it can mean near annihilation of the human race. The change came with the development of nuclear weapons. The strength of weapons has always determined the potential damage that could be done to groups of people. When we had only rocks and sticks to throw at each other, the potential group damage from a dispute was minimal. Hand-to-hand combat has always been dangerous to individuals, but seldom terminal for entire nations. As the weapons progressed in power, so did the number of individuals who could be harmed in combat and the extent of their injuries. The human race now has nuclear weapons, which cannot restrain the number of people affected. Nuclear weapons are made because the technology is available and because the hunger for political dominance goes unchecked. When the first atomic bomb was made, there was little or no pre-thinking about a nuclear arms race. There was next to no prophetic forecasting about the affect on international relations or on national budget implications. No, the military brass then engaged in combat saw the bomb's effects in the context of World War II or others like it. But "The Bomb" became an inextricable part of our lives, and now we cannot envision another war like World War II. Any future war on a global scale will be much more devastating, and, almost inevitably, centered around the use of nuclear weapons. This is inevitable because all are not likely to impose limitations on their power.

This all leads back where we started: Christians limiting their own power. When Christians organize to switch from single-issue politics and candidate evaluation on the basis of their own worldview to electing a religious celebrity as president of the United States, we move from normal combat into "nuclear politics." Moderation is not the point or the possibility. The power in the presidency is an all-or-nothing power. Even though the long-term effects of a person's presidency may be minimal in history, the long-term effects of a religious celebrity as president on Christianity might be disastrous. It is not possible for a president to stay out of the spotlight. It is not likely that a religious celebrity will say things that are taken as unimportant. Once he says it, it will be taken as a religious dictum for everyone. The combination of the power of the presidency with the power of a nationally recognized religious leader needs much forethought. The "nuclear politics" involved would cost Christianity as the nuclear arms race has cost America. The escalation has taken resources away from more constructive purposes. The suspicion generated has become as fearful as the bomb itself. And the need to borrow from our future has made our future frightening.

No, the way to avoid entering nuclear politics is to avoid combining the top office of the state and a top office of religion. We should restrain ourselves to lesser offices and issues, to lesser forms of influence.

So we choose not to elect an evangelical celebrity to the presidency—and limit ourselves politically to individual influence rather than group imperialism. The political expression of individuals' personal beliefs makes for the healthy operation of both our political system and our Christian witness. Individuals who agree upon certain issues acting in unified ways may gain political influence. But an individual who is said to represent Christianity in politics moves toward dominance (sin). To imply that an individual would have representational powers for Christianity would be natural for the world but deceptive for Protestant Christianity. In Protestant theology, no individual can represent Christendom. There is one possibility of an individual operating as a perceived representative of Christianity, thus threatening attempted religious dominance, and that is to elect a recognized religious leader. On the other hand, an individual speaking consistently with religious integrity stays attached to the Spirit and disengaged from Christendom's temptation toward political domination. There is one possibility of an individual operating as a Christian in office (in the same way other Christians operate in their jobs), and that is the possibility of electing an evangelical lay person who has been called to a ministry of service in government.

The desire for dominance must be kept separate from the state, the instrument of coercion. Whether the sin is attempted in reality or only in the imagination of the world, the effects would be the same: an impediment to our spiritual witness in the future and the compromise of our place in the present. Christianity is on historical record as being no more effective in political government than others, and even less tolerant than others (the religious governments in the early colonies were *not* tolerant of other religions—not even other Christian denominations). Christianity acted out in the life of an individual, however, is the most powerful influence in the world, in or out of political office. Now the question is simply whether we would rather influence or dominate.

Notes

1. Walter Rauschenbusch, A *Theology for the Social Gospel* (New York: Macmillan, 1917), 142.
2. "The National Election," *Radical Religion*, Winter 1936, 142.
3. Arthur Schlesinger, Jr., "Reinhold Niebuhr's Role in Political Thought," in *Reinhold Niebuhr: His Religious, Social, and Political Thought*, ed. Charles Kegley and Robert Bretall (New York: Macmillan, 1956), 149.
4. W. Penfield, "Memory Mechanisms," AMA *Archives of Neurology and Psychiatry*, vol. 67 (1952), 178-198.
5. Reinhold Niebuhr, *Moral Man and Immoral Society* (New York: Scribner's, 1932), 117.
6. M. Scott Peck, *People of the Lie* (New York: Simon and Schuster, 1983), 216.

PART II

After Analysis, Action

God save us from hotheads
who would lead us foolishly,
and from cold feet that would
keep us from adventuring
at all.

PETER MARSHALL

SIX

Thinking Democracy, Thinking Righteousness

Liberty without obedience is confusion, and obedience without liberty is slavery.

William Penn

Part I of this book emphasized caution about "Christian politics." Its theme was that we should not swallow the simplistic myth that we have done our duty if we elect godly principals to high office. Part II will focus on a different tactic: if we can have an electorate of godly principals doing their duty, the government will reflect more godly principles naturally. Our job is not to convert the government, it is to convert ourselves. The Bible is not as concerned with how religious a government is; rather the concern is how righteous the people become in response to the government. The *people* are the objective.

The first step in this understanding is to reread the Scriptures with a God-government theme in mind. We are like a layperson who was asked to lead a worship service. Although he had been sitting through the same worship format for years, he came the next Sunday with a notepad. He explained, "I once came to receive leadership in my worship experience. If I am going to be called to give leadership, I need to look at the same thing through different eyes." Yes, if we common folk are going to be called to leadership, we need to take a look at the Scriptures with different eyes.

The Importance and Unimportance of Structure

Though the Old Testament and New Testament are quite different in presenting the way God leads His people, the intention of God is always the same. He desires to be our God and desires us to be His people (Isa. 43:21). That desire may be accomplished through different forms of government, but not through anarchy (Jude 5-8). God will use some form of government to provide an environment in which we may come to Him. God has used different forms of governments and has worked His purpose in each (Dan. 2:21). Yet the human governments themselves are limited in their importance to God (Isa. 40:15, 17, 23-25), because He is sovereign in their existence (Isa. 41:2-4).

The forms He used in the Old Testament period varied much more than the civil government forms used in the New Testament. The Spirit, likewise, was poured out differently. A quick overview of history can highlight the changes in governmental form. When God called forth a people to be under His direct leadership (Gen. 12:1-3), the patriarchal structure of the family sufficed for government. No special anointing for leadership was mentioned, no elaboration of structure was given. A son of the patriarchal government, Joseph, found himself a leader in another type of civil government, and God used that pagan government to accomplish His purpose (Gen. 50:20). Just as God uses a believer in a nonbelievers' government, so also He uses a believer *against* that government. With Moses we see that He calls people to another form of government, with His appointed leader and purpose. He does direct Moses, eventually, to rely upon a more elaborate structure with the Law (Exod. 20), the priesthood (Exod. 19:22), and the court system (Deut. 1:12-17). Then during the period of the judges we see God raise up temporary leaders, effective in short-term government but made ineffectual in the long run by the peoples' unrighteousness. In hindsight, we see the general spiritual principle of government written in Proverbs 14:34: "Righteousness exalts a nation, but sin is a disgrace to any people." Later, despite God's warning, Israel demands a king (1 Sam. 8) as a substitute for God's direct kingship over their lives. God anoints Kings Saul, David, and Solomon to unite the kingdom, and also raises up prophets like Nathan to confront perversions in government (2 Sam. 12:1-14). During the ensuing period of the divided kingdom and corrupt kings, God continues to use the voice of prophets to correct or confront government. Following that period, God even used captivity by a foreign government (2 Kings 15:29; 17:6) as part of His government of Israel. Foreign kings became His instruments (Isa. 45:1) and Israel learns the cost of inattentiveness. After the Babylonian captivity, Israel returns to a civil government dominated by various foreign powers, except for a brief period under the Maccabees (Jewish leaders who rededicated the temple). The last dominant power noted in Scripture is the Roman Empire.

It is during the post-exilic period that separation of religion and state becomes a necessity for ongoing life. Spiritual authority is only loosely connected with government. The Jews and, later, Christians are too devoted to their faith to look to the state for the ultimate leadership in their lives. During Christ's time, Rome delegated certain religious and civil authority to the Sanhedrin, the Jewish ruling council. During this period provincial civil rulers, like Pontius Pilate, had ultimate but tenuous authority. To keep the peace and, therefore, his job, the provincial ruler had to pay attention to the independence-minded Jewish religious leaders. In time, however, the Jews had no religious input into civil government. Jerusalem was destroyed in A.D 70, and the civil government both completely dominated and periodically persecuted the Christians.

God, we believe, moves in mysterious ways. We even believe that He was working in the various forms of government.

He is a flexible God, one Who does not, obviously, depend on one standard form to achieve His ends.

Biblical Principles and Civil Governments

Now that we see that God has used many forms of government to work out His purposes, we may be released from a nagging suspicion that if we just got the form of government right the Spirit would be able to work. In the different forms of government the Spirit is constantly at work, bringing God's people to Him. However, God is recorded as alternately working through, in spite of, or against certain governments. Though God uses all governments for His ultimate purpose, He does not react the same toward all governments—and neither will the people who follow Him. There are at least five reactions to civil governments given in Scripture.

Obedience. Obedience is the primary reaction in Scripture. Our God is a God of order. To eliminate chaos He has put certain structures into our lives. They reflect His nature and our need for order. They also test whether we can learn the most valuable trait in following God—submission. If we cannot submit to what we have seen, how can we submit to what we have not seen? For these reasons Romans 13:1-2 states, "Let every person be in subjection to the governing authorities. For there is no authority except from God, and those which exist are established by God. Therefore he who resists authority has opposed the ordinance of God." Notice the connection between civil and spiritual submission. Governments teach us something that has spiritual significance: we cannot always have our own way. Our reaction to earthly authority certainly indicates our reaction to heavenly authority. If we respond positively to authority, it means we recognize the necessity of structure. The structure of civil government keeps us safe from each other and foreign threats. Paul, in 1 Timothy 2:1-2, requests prayer for governing authorities "in order that we may lead a tranquil and quiet life." With our basic need for security met, we are free to turn our attention and energies toward the meaning of life.

Civil government is just one of the structures of the universe necessary for accumulating meaningful purpose. A strong marriage will permit freedom and development in the individual partners. A strong sense of parental stability gives a child the foundation needed to explore the world. Secure employment gives the employee the ability to focus on family, friends, and ministry. Just as the structure in music frees the notes to vary and create beauty, so the stronger structures in our lives allow us freedom to be creative. Maintenance of the structures of life is a minimal investment of time for the return of security and stability they give. Christians in politics are our investment in maintaining the structure of civil government. Christians obeying that structure of government are paying the minimal daily requirement for getting on with the real substance of life.

Repentance. Repentance can be an appropriate reaction to government. If God's concern is the nearness of His people to Him, He may allow disruptions in the structures of society (including government) as a sign to repent. In 2 Chronicles 7:13-14, God plainly states, "If I send pestilence among My people, and My people who are called by My name humble themselves and pray, and seek My face and turn from their wicked ways, then I will hear from heaven, will forgive their sin, and will heal their land." Christians, then, can use even the worst forms of government as a cause for self-examination and spiritual growth. Too often our reflex is to try to fix the pestilence before we fix ourselves. An excellent question to ask ourselves in response to a government's inadequacies is, "How can I use this 'pestilence' to help me depend upon God rather than government and change my life for the better?" All forms of government should spur us to godly behavior (Rom. 13:3-5) so that God's will may "be done on earth as it is in heaven." A Christian involved in politics should have personal reform rather than government reform as a primary agenda.

Civil Disobedience. Having stated the need for personal repentance, we must also recognize there are times when civil disobedience is the appropriate reaction to a governmental edict. The obvious example is Acts 4:18-20, when believers were ordered to do what was directly opposed to what they knew to be right. "And when they had summoned them [the apostles], they commanded them not to speak or teach at all in the name of Jesus. But Peter and John answered and said to them, 'Whether it is right in the sight of God to give heed to you rather than to God, you be the judge; for we cannot stop speaking what we have seen and heard.'" The same dynamic is reported in Acts 5:29 where the apostles state flatly, "We must obey God rather than men." Civil disobedience was Daniel's witness also. The important aspect of biblical civil disobedience is its *motivation*. It is done when there is a direct conflict between what the government would force an individual to do and what God would have him do. It is not an attempt at government reform so much as it is a personal moral necessity. It is not a matter of having one's rights violated; it is a matter of being forced to do what is wrong. Therefore, though Scripture validates civil disobedience, it does not see it as a political tool. Rather, civil disobedience is a last stand against a perverted government, a stand that includes accepting the punishment. A good question to screen an act of civil disobedience is, "Is this disobedience a witness against a government action that forces me and others to do wrong, or is it simply a strategy to gain political power?" In the first instance, one is obeying a greater structure of the universe—moral law. In the second instance, one may be putting self above obeying any structure, and that is not a Christian's option.

Correction. Correction (not rebellion) is a biblical response to government. In the Old Testament there are many instances where God sent a prophet to challenge the direction of a government (1 Kings 12:21-24, for example). In the New Testament, John the Baptist tried to correct Herod (Matt. 14:4) and was killed because of it. Yet not all corrections of government took the form of confrontations. Esther and Joseph were two believers who became a part of the government personnel and had a profound effect on policy. Their participation in government made a distinct difference in the civil government's attitude toward God's people. Paul progressed through the Roman judicial system (Acts 25:11) with a goal of influencing people for Christ as he went (Acts 26:27-29). His goal was to make a difference in the lives of political officeholders. Paul, like other biblical figures, was someone who could have been an enemy of the government, but instead was a friend who offered a correction in course. Scripture pictures reproof as a part of love (Prov. 3:12) and as a real help to the wise (Prov. 9:8; 10:17; 12:1; 13:18; 15:5).

Americans are both blessed and challenged by living under a political system that demands correction in its development. Our Constitution is a developing document. It will be interpreted and amended over the years according to the character of the nation. Our democracy depends upon correction as circumstances change. Unlike a totalitarian system that must defend itself against change, democracy theoretically calls for mid-course correction via input from the people. So the reaction of correction is not only modeled in Scripture, it is necessary in our system of government.

Transplanting. Transplanting is another scriptural reaction to government, and it is the most complicated. When a Christian is living under a government which he finds most ungodly, he may find that neither civil disobedience nor correction is an appropriate option. The logical choice is rebellion, but rebellion is not a scriptural option. There is simply no way to reconcile the concepts of rebellion and submission to the governing authorities.

Rebellion is a form of anarchy, which is the complete absence of government and law. Anarchy is a state where each individual goes his own way and chaos reigns. It violates the structure of the universe and the nature of God. God holds anarchy in such abhorrence that His servant, Joshua, advises people to serve false gods rather than no God: "If it is disagreeable in your sight to serve the Lord, choose for yourselves today whom you will serve: whether the gods which your fathers served which were beyond the River, or the gods of the Amorites in whose land you are living; but as for me and my house, we will serve the Lord" (Josh. 24:15). Anarchy exalts the individual to the status of a god and precludes any form of submission except that which comes from human whim.

The first (and sometimes last) step toward anarchy is rebellion. Rebellion is the nonsubmission to authority while pretending to live under that authority. Rebellion is the individual raising himself above the government or placing himself outside the law. Rebellion is not *for* anything else, it is just *against* what is. It is purely negative, and there is no kind word for it in Scripture. What, then, is a scriptural answer for those who feel compelled to be against an evil government? They must be against the evil government from without, not from within. If attempting open correction is not an option, and civil disobedience is not necessary, then the believer must be transplanted to be submissive to a different authority.

In Matthew 2:13, we read of an evil government that demands the life of the infant Jesus. Neither correction nor civil disobedience was an appropriate reaction to that government. So "an angel of the Lord appeared to Joseph in a dream, saying, 'Arise and take the Child and His mother, and flee to Egypt, and remain there until I tell you; for Herod is going to search for the Child to destroy Him.'" In this case Joseph, Mary, and the child were transplanted under a civil government that took no issue with the government from which they had come; the agenda was simply safety. A like circumstance is described in Matthew 10:23, where Jesus is instructing His disciples, "But whenever they persecute you in this city, flee to the next." The act of transplanting from one set of city fathers to the next is not one of government reform, it is a strategy for safety and continuing ministry. The respect for and submission to a civil government is still a part of the individual's life, but, in an effort to continue his life and ministry, he leaves the country. This biblical strategy would work toward the ideal that any person ought to be able to leave a country for the purposes of life or ministry.

Our own American Revolution looked like pure rebellion, but it was actually the birth of a new nation. The Declaration of Independence clearly separated the people from English authority. The Constitution completed that separation by instituting a legitimate civil government. After attempted correction, the next step was transplantation by creation of a new governmental authority. Because of the geographic separation, the colonies were somewhat predisposed toward self-government. In many ways the American people had already begun to form an identity and government separate from Britain. The "taxation without representation" issue was more an evidence of a separate ethos and people than of subjects who wanted more involvement in British government.

Each of the above reactions to government is rooted in respect for, and the need for, authority. No matter what the form of government, Christians are called to recognize the necessity of government. Now let us build our understanding of our particular responsibility to our own government.

A Holy Scriptural Principle

One concept in the Bible is critical in determining appropriate action for Christians in many areas, including politics. The concept has not been used much in a practical way because it has not been understood completely by the general Christian populace. When most Christians are asked about scriptural guidelines for Christian involvement in government, we make a beeline to a Bible concordance or a topical index. We proceed to look up *government* or *authority* or *citizenship*. We then attempt to tie the pack of principles we have found into some semblance of order. We sense the need for an overarching principle to help us interpret and order the various passages, but we can't seem to pull one out of the pack. Well, there is such a principle. It is just not in "the pack." *The principle is the biblical concept of righteousness.* The word *righteousness* may click the reader into some automatic response of holy head-nodding or enthusiastic anticipation of lambasting the evils of society. Such reflexes show how misunderstood the concept is. Righteousness is actually a practical concept, helpful in everyday ways. Let us first define it accurately, then apply it to Christians in politics.

The best definition of righteousness I have ever read was also the simplest. Doctors Elizabeth and Paul Achtemeier, Old and New Testament scholars respectively, sum up the scriptural definition of righteousness in this way: "The fulfillment of the demands of a relationship, whether with men or with God."[1] If the reader will look up different passages containing the word *righteousness* in the Bible, he will not only see that this is an accurate definition, but it also points to practical application.

It is strange that the concept of righteousness is so often used in the Bible and so seldom used by us. Part of our clumsiness in handling this important concept is our confusion as to what it really means. Many of us have assumed righteousness to be a synonym for holiness, or goodness, or moralism. In fact, it is quite different than each of these. Holiness implies a separation, a withdrawal from common use; righteousness implies not separation but linking in relationship. Goodness has a Hebrew root meaning of "pleasant." It is a positive, beneficent term, but not specific. Righteousness, on the other hand, is only operative in specifics. Moralism is the offensive twin of goodness. Goodness intimates; moralism intimidates. Moralism commands behavior in universal absolutes; it is the answer waiting in ambush for a question. Righteousness, however, arises from relationships where persons as well as questions are addressed, and respect as well as an answer are given.

It may surprise many to know that biblical righteousness is not a matter of universal standards but of particular relationship. The Old Testament is consistent with the New Testament: the context of righteousness is a specific relationship. When Abraham "believed in the Lord; and He reckoned it to him as righteousness" (Gen. 15:6), we see the forming of a specific relationship. Faith, not performance nor obeying the rules of the universe, was what brought Abraham into relationship with a personal God. Faith was what God wanted. According to Paul's writing in Galatians, Christ was sent to relieve us of a bondage to some cold, universal standard of behavior (what the Law had become) and restore us to a trusting relationship with God. The relationship fulfills God's nature of love: "We love, because He first loved us" (1 John 4:19). Furthermore, God is continually described as righteous in Scripture, but it has nothing to do with His meeting up to ethical standards that are outside of Him and judge Him. His righteousness is always in terms of His care for us in the needs of our relationship to Him. Even further, when Scripture speaks of "man to man" righteousness, the standards met are the ones of the particular relationships. In Matthew 25:31-46, notice that the specific needs are responded to in kind. The "righteous" are not responding to any exterior ethical standards. They apparently are not even aware that it is a simultaneous response to men and God until He explains it to them. In overview, relationship is so primary that the law itself is summarized not in terms of behavior, but in terms of love (Matt. 22:36-40). So righteousness is not identical with written morality, coded ethics, or religious norms, except as they proceed naturally from a relationship.

Taken one step further, righteousness in the New Testament presumes a relationship that needs the active participation of both parties for its preservation. Christians may recognize this as a description of a *covenant* relationship. By living up to the responsibilities of a particular covenant relationship, one is seen as fulfilling righteousness. While all Christians are deemed righteous in Christ because we have fulfilled the demands of our relationship to God in Him, we have yet to act righteously in specific and various situations. Fulfilling the demands of various relationships is how we act out that righteousness. So righteousness is a responsive activity, fulfilling the demands of any relationship, but especially called forth in a covenant relationship. The determinant is not how expressly religious one is in the relationship, but whether or not one has kept the trust of the relationship. Every relationship is valuable to God, whether it is explicitly religious or not, and our obligations in each relationship are to be fulfilled (Matt. 5:33-37). The obligations, or demands, will of course vary from relationship to relationship and from time to time. What is righteous in one relationship might not be righteous in another. It may be our obligation to tell our children what to do; it may not be our obligation to tell our friends what to do. What is righteous at one time in a relationship may not be righteous at another time in that relationship. It may be righteous to ask your five-year-old if he has brushed his teeth; his maturity level and your teaching responsibility demands that. It is probably not righteous for you to call your forty-five-year-old son each morning to ask the same question.

So the biblical principle of righteousness requires us to fulfill the demands of each relationship as is appropriate. The relationship need not have an explicit religious purpose to be the context for righteousness. The attentive father or mother, the conscientious worker, the servant leader, the helpful friend, the loving spouse, and the voting citizen are all being righteous. While moral absolutes exist, the value of relationships is the point of righteousness. Universal standards for behavior in all relationships exist, but righteousness begins with an appropriate behavior in a particular relationship. As Proverbs 15:28 says, "The heart of the righteous ponders how to answer." Righteousness thrives in covenant relationships where demands are clarified, agreed upon, and binding.

When we find and keep valid demands in a relationship, we fulfill the righteousness God has imputed to us in Christ.

The Righteous American

Among our many relationships is the one with our government. All Christians have a responsibility to relate to the government that has authority over them (Rom. 13:1-7). United States citizens are bound in a unique and positive way to a special form of government.

There are several reasons why Christians are reluctant to take an active place in steering our government. Some people believe that civil government deals with worldly issues and such are not the Christian's concern. They believe that the kingdom of God is the antithesis of the evil world and, therefore, they should separate themselves from such worldly concerns. In a sense, many are like our brothers and sisters in the Amish tradition. Stick with the horse and buggy, because once you start involvement with the things of the world, it is difficult to draw the line.

Some other Christians just have no interest whatsoever in political issues. They are very glad to take the passenger's seat. Wherever they are driven, within reason, is fine with them. They just have no attraction toward that steering wheel.

Others could have an interest, but the demands of all the other relationships they have are overwhelming. They just do not have the time to consider one more thing—especially something as huge as politics. They would say, "You drive, because I have four things I need to get done between here and wherever we are going."

Some people have never seriously considered politics before and are afraid to start now. They believe that the issues are too complex to ever understand. Or they may be so disgusted with politics that they won't participate "because it doesn't make any difference." There are dozens of understandable reasons why people avoid responsible involvement in our political process. There are also a few bad reasons, like laziness. But there are no righteous reasons for not taking some responsibility in our government, because our government demands that we participate as our part of the relationship.

We owe our government. When Jesus said, "Then render to Caesar the things that are Caesar's; and to God the things that are God's," He was giving more than one-time advice. He was stating the principle of righteousness. We are to pay what the government demands, not just in taxes, but in participation. Inasmuch as we threw patriotism out the window in the 1960s because of some valid concerns about the Vietnam War, we threw the proverbial baby out with the bathwater. There is a place in the Bible for giving to the government what is due because God can work in us and in government through that involvement. What, then, does the United States government demand of us?

Loyalty. In gleaning concepts from our most important government documents, the Declaration of Independence and the Constitution, we may note at least four demands our government makes of us. The first demand is one of *loyalty.* The last sentence of the Declaration of Independence announces both a reliance upon God and an attachment to each other as requirements for continued freedom: "And, for the support of this declaration, with a firm reliance on the protection of Divine Providence, we mutually pledge to each other our lives, our fortunes, and our sacred honour." The mutual pledge to each other is more than a nice promise. It gives us more than security. Indeed, our loyalty to this nation and its government is necessary for the country's continued existence. It is the task of every government to enlist the support of the majority of its people. That consistent support, or loyalty, is what makes government a legitimate agent of the people instead of a coercive force on the people. The very nature of a democracy presupposes both genuine interest and faithfulness on the part of its people. The loyalty does not mean being a yes-man to every government policy. Quite the contrary, democracy depends upon loyalty beyond whatever answer or comment we have. Agreement is not necessary, but fidelity is. No government can be considered stable, much less effective, without the willing allegiance of its citizens. Our democracy can only be strong if we fulfill the demand of staying true to it as contrasted to any other worldly government or no worldly government at all. As long as we live as United States citizens, we owe this government our loyalty as part of righteousness.

Tolerance. The second thing our government requires is *tolerance*. Again, in the Declaration of Independence we read that "all men are created equal; that they are endowed by their Creator with certain unalienable rights; that among these are life, liberty, and the pursuit of happiness. That, to secure these rights, governments are instituted among men." These enduring words of wisdom do not mention tolerance, but tolerance is the summary of them. If all men are created equal, does not another's opinion have as much place as mine? Truth is not a requirement for a hearing in a democracy. Practically every reader will agree with this general concept. When surveyed, at least 75 percent of the electorate supported the general democratic values. The percentage "ranged from a low of 77 percent who agreed that freedom of conscience should include the freedom to be an atheist, to a high of 94.3 percent who agreed that no matter what a person's political beliefs are, he is entitled to the same legal rights and protections as anyone else . . . [but] when these general statements were translated into specific terms, the consensus disappeared."[2] Therein lies a real problem. Americans value differences and are quite proud of the fact that all people are free to hold their own beliefs. And the tendency is growing. The Gallup Report (October 1985) states that one of the most notable changes in those surveyed over the last fifty years has been the growth in tolerance. Yet experience tells us that trouble occurs when general fundamental values are translated into specific legislation or concrete action. We like the ideal of tolerance, but we dislike having to actually use tolerance.

Tolerance is a demand from our government from two perspectives. Our system of government will not work without the minority possessing equal rights. The majority must prevail, but it must be a reasonable prevailing. Without the protection of the law, the minority could be oppressed by the majority. Oppression, it should be remembered, is no more admirable when it comes from a majority than it is when it comes from a despot. Tolerance is the heart of the minority's reasonable protection. Without a basic attitude of tolerance, laws and courts can drift from the democratic ideal. Additionally, the very integrity of political activism itself depends on a basic atmosphere of tolerance. One reason why relatively few Americans are politically active is their fear of conflict and rejection. Many see political disagreement as a form of violence they would be glad to avoid. An atmosphere of tolerance, emanating from people dedicated to understanding and reconciliation, is a prerequisite for most Americans' involvement. The democratic ideal envisions people who can and do disagree but are reasonable in their expression of that disagreement and respectful of their adversaries.

Understanding. The third demand our government makes on us is that of *understanding*. Of course, understanding does much to promote tolerance. Most political science research indicates that those who best understand democratic principles and political issues are the most tolerant. But the need for understanding goes beyond tolerance. Understanding is the very basis of democracy, which calls for its citizens to be rulers as well as subjects. In contrast to some political systems that require only submission on the part of their subjects, democracy calls for leadership on the part of its citizens. The leadership may come through representatives elected, political action coalitions, individual influence, or a combination of all these and more. The theory, though, is clear about the objective: the people will rule. Again, the words of the Declaration of Independence speak of governments "deriving their just powers from the consent of the governed." Even as government derives its just powers from citizens, citizens derive their powers of justice from understanding. None of us can well pretend to fulfill the role of citizen-ruler without understanding. When our system of government calls upon us for involvement, it assumes that in our involvement we will make reasoned choices from among many alternatives for the public good. That assumption, which underlies all democratic theory, raises several significant questions. Am I making my choice on someone's recommendation, or do I understand the issue myself? Am I taking on my role as ruler (voter) on the basis of emotion or a well thought out decision? How many alternatives have I considered? Why is the other side for the other side? What is the public good in this case as differentiated from my own good or my group's good?

Involvement. The fourth demand that our government theoretically places upon us is one of *action* or *involvement*. The preamble to the Constitution of the United States of America states very clearly, "We the people of the United States . . . do . . ." Our government was established by the people and depends upon the involvement of the people. Yet more voters turn out on election day in totalitarian than in democratic countries, and in no other major democratic nation is participation at the polls so poor as in the United States. Sixty percent of the eligible electorate is considered a good turnout in presidential elections, and in local elections it often goes as low as 10 percent.[3] Isn't it interesting that those who have the most power exercise it least, and that the elections in which we could have the most direct role (local), we are involved least of all? There are many reasons why this is so; some have been listed, others need to be discovered. The point we must stick to here, however, is that a participatory democracy presumes involvement by masses of the people it serves. They play an important role in making policy and in holding the government responsible for its actions. Their participation will not only guide government but limit it. It is the involvement of the people that insures the healthy competition so necessary to balance and choice. Without involvement by all, power accumulates in too concentrated a form, in too few hands, in too narrow a perspective. Opposition is not a hindrance to progress; it is necessary to progress. It refines and purifies. It offers correctives. It promises problems in the future if we don't build relationships today. The ideal of involvement insures that neither the single-issue impassioned person nor the every-issue addict will dominate the system. Democracy calls for the people who are not extremely interested nor dogmatically decided to come into the arena, if only periodically. Otherwise we have, by default, government by political aristocracy or oligarchy. Those who think that is what we may have now need to read on.

Two Philosophies—One Course

The second simple factor in determining our social responsibility lies in deciding that it is as much our calling to be involved as it is our congressmen's. "All of this is ideally true," someone may say, "but there is a big difference in the way American democracy is supposed to work and the way it actually works. I've never been involved, except for voting when I can, and the country seems to be doing fine. Maybe it works better when there are only a few involved. Why rock the boat? Let us be practical. If it's not broken, I'm not going to spend time trying to fix it. Now what do you say to that?"

That is a perfectly understandable line of thinking. Perhaps the needs of our government are in reality quite a bit less than the ideals it puts forth. In fact, if every voter were loyal to the point of being informed and involved, would that not overload the system?

The proposition that our democracy works best when most of the voting public remains apathetic has some merit. It is recognized by most political scientists that the qualities needed to operate a democratic system smoothly are not as likely found in the average voter as in those who love politics. The average voter, it is argued, is much more likely to see his political involvement as a crusade to win benefits for himself, rather than being open to what is best for society. The average voter seems less likely to see compromise as a valuable option for progress, to recognize that government needs constant improvement, to value the variety of others' opinions. The case for the average voter to remain uninvolved also assumes that our political situation is much too complicated for most to understand, therefore the pressure for simplistic solutions would increase with his involvement. In other words, the argument is that the average voter is not well-informed about the democratic principles necessary for efficient government functioning. The argument further presumes that those political people who are naturally attracted to become deeply involved have all of the qualities that the average voter is missing. The conclusion, then, is that the natural evolvement of apathy has worked to everyone's benefit.

There is, of course, as strong an argument on the other side of this issue. It would propose that the average voter *does* have the intelligence to understand the complexity of most issues, *does* possess the practicality to operate within the system as it is, and *does* have the capacity to see beyond his own cause. The argument could go on indefinitely. The point here is not which case is stronger. The point here is one that Christians constantly face: do we try to bring ideals down to reality, or do we try to bring reality up to the ideal?

The demands of American democracy remain the same whether the average citizen meets them or not. If righteousness fulfills the demands of the relationship, the proceeding arguments are unimportant. The question is, Am I going to try to fulfill those demands (loyalty, tolerance, understanding, involvement) or not? Democracy, like Christianity, was never meant to be just an ideal—it was meant to be a norm. The question cannot be confined to how well the system is working. The concern must be broadened and deepened to what difference it makes in the lives of the individuals. Yes, the ideal is impossible to accomplish—that is what makes it an ideal. Each citizen will not stay informed, involved, or tolerant. Perhaps some will not even remain loyal. Yet making perfect citizens is not the Christian's agenda. Our agenda is making the government's demand of every citizen normative in our own lives.

Notes

1. P. J. Achtemeier, "Righteousness in the Old Testament," *The Interpreter's Dictionary of the Bible*, vol. 4 (Nashville: Abingdon, 1962), 80, 91.
2. John Livingston and Robert Thompson, *The Consent of the Governed* (New York: Macmillan, 1966), 293.
3. Ibid., 295.

SEVEN

The Pilate Program, Part 1: Seeing What's in Front of Us

It is not the role of government to judge between rival systems of metaphysics and to legislate one among others. Rather, government's role is to protect and preserve a free course for its constitutional guarantees.

Carl F. H. Henry

I have wondered if being a Christian in politics and being Christlike in politics is the same. I think not. *Christian* is the name of a representative group. We are a group with vested interests in the world, interests that make it difficult for us to be objective. Christ was interested in the world—which is not the same as having interests (to be protected) in the world. Christ could look at the world and be interested primarily in the spiritual welfare of all individuals. Christians look at the world and see "us" and "them."

There are probably many Christian approaches to politics. I would assume from the political involvement of most Christians I have seen that their strategy is identical with non-Christian groups. We Christians tend to focus on an issue or candidate, match that person to our value system, accumulate a power base in reaction, and do what we can for or against. That is how politics works, and that seems to be how Christian politics works. Perhaps there is a difference afterward in the way the country runs; perhaps not. But is there a difference afterward in the way people view Christ? Perhaps Christians have more respect and power after a political battle; perhaps not. But is their reflection on God one that becomes Him, and is their witness one with which He is pleased?

There would be great advantage in finding a Christlike approach to politics. The advantage would not necessarily be for the Christians, but, when all was said and done, it would glorify God. Just as the scriptural principle of righteousness makes it clear that we must be involved, we also need a scriptural program of how to be involved. *But "scriptural program" here means learning from Scripture instead of just quoting Scripture.* Certainly any Christian approach would be within the guidelines of Scripture. But a Christlike approach will not emphasize guidelines nearly as much as relationships. Establishing "Christian values" was not the goal of Christ; people were and are His goal. Love is so much more difficult than being right. Any so-called Christian approach to politics that emphasizes victory more than love is just another play for power.

A Christian approach to politics could well show the opposition just how wrong that opposition is. The Christlike approach to politics could well show the opposition just how worthy of love and respect those opposition people are. A Christian approach could tell everyone how to vote; the Christlike approach could invite everyone to look for God in the political situation before us. A Christian approach could give us certainty; the Christlike approach could give us insight.

It seems reasonable, when investigating how to face politics in a Christlike manner, to turn to the record of the main event in which Christ faced politics. In returning to that event we can extract a picture of Christ's approach, Pilate's mistakes, and God's success. With that picture in mind we can discern a practical approach to address every political situation. I call this "The Pilate Program" to remind us how we often miss the point of political confrontations. Its basic objective is to give individuals a means to approach issues or candidates in ways that will not miss the point. The Pilate Program will help us determine what we believe, why we believe it, and why we believe it is of God. The practical result will be that many individuals will be able to become both competent and Christlike in a political setting. The government will not only sense a large Christian grassroots concern; the population will see a selfless political approach. What a witness that would be!

But Identify with Pilate?

Some of us will have difficulty identifying with Pilate. After all, he was not very much like us, was he? Well, maybe a few of his more obvious traits will sound familiar. As we read Matthew 27:11-26, Mark 15:1-15, Luke 23:1-25, and John 18:28–19:22, we may identify with some of his tendencies. First, even though Pilate was in the position of being politically responsible, he was not at all excited about addressing religiopolitical issues. He was not looking for trouble; his life seemed best when the status quo was maintained. He had plenty to do and was not searching for additional items to put on his agenda. When confronted with this religiopolitical issue, this candidate for king of the Jews, he knew it was his job to decide the case. But he decided to avoid deciding. He put it back upon the religious people who had raised the issue in the first place. They were the ones with the heartburn, he assumed, so let them take care of the matter: "Take Him yourselves, and judge Him" (John 18:31). But they tossed the matter back to him, claiming that they alone could not do what needed to be done. Pilate then tried to pass the matter on to Herod (Luke 23:7-12). Herod stamped "Return to Sender" on the case. If the religiously agitated couldn't handle the matter, and if the rest of the political system avoided the matter, maybe it was Pilate's responsibility to decide. So he did decide, but he did not take responsibility. He let custom tender his decision

(Matt. 27:15). He let the crowd reverse his judgment (Luke 23:16, 25). He let excuse replace action (Matt. 27:24).

Perhaps Pilate is not so different from us in his avoidance of the religiopolitical issues. We who are citizen-rulers avoid those issues because they are so much trouble. We tend to leave it to our beloved political system or to a majority who neither recognizes nor cares about Christ. We may say, "I'll leave it to the religious activists, since they are so interested," only to have them say, "We need your help." Our reasons for avoidance may be similar to Pilate's also.

Pilate had a tendency to fear what might happen to his relationships if he were involved in religious politics. He had family pressure not to get involved (Matt. 27:19). There could be job repercussions if he were connected with such controversial matters (John 19:12). Pilate was also getting all stirred up inside; his peace with himself was challenged (John 19:7-8). It is no wonder that Pilate dreaded religiopolitical issues, nor that we do. Some of those issues may demand a price far greater than we are willing to pay. That is our choice, as it was Pilate's. But like Pilate, we are from time to time confronted with such situations. We can learn much from his mistakes and even more from Christ's example. Let us now turn to the six-step Christian political approach called the Pilate Program.

Detaching the Demonstration

I define a *demonstration* as one or more people confronting us with a political issue. The confrontation has the effect of arousing our emotions and capturing our attention. For Pilate, both Jesus, the controversial religious leader, and the mob who brought Christ were demonstrations.

The primary step in addressing religiopolitical situations is to calm down to an atmosphere that will permit reason. Like booster rockets, demonstrations tend to perform one valuable act. They boost a singular issue above the other issues into a place where all can see and pay attention. Like booster rockets, demonstrations have one major liability: after they have done their work, they are dead weight. The aircraft should detach that booster rocket after the booster has done its job.

When the demonstration resides in a single controversial person, like a religious celebrity running for political office, the demonstration is impossible to detach from the person. The demonstration *is* the person. Every time we see him we are so strongly reminded of particular political concerns that he is to us a confrontation rather than a candidate. Because he is a demonstration, everything that happens will appear to be a demonstration of Christianity (inflation, spending, deficit, etc.). For example, when Pat Robertson was thinking of running for president, two "Americans for Robertson" came on a local "call-in" radio program. Their aim was to respond to questions people might have about where Dr. Robertson stood on any particular issue. For the entire call-in period, however, people called to respond to his religion. They were particularly fixed on that one issue that he so strongly represented to them. Despite repeated pleas to the audience to call in with questions about other campaign issues, no one did. Religion was the repeated theme. The two representatives from Robertson's campaign headquarters sounded both frustrated and exhausted by the end of the program. They had not been able to detach Robertson's ministry from his candidacy. Like anyone who reaches the status of major religious figure (Jesus included), Robertson's religious image was so potent it would not permit a regular, reasonable deliberation. That image sparked a nondetachable demonstration in people's minds that engendered more passion than thought. Therefore, it was almost inevitable that people would overreact positively or negatively to the person, instead of calmly to the issues.

Pilate discovered how inflammatory a situation can become when a major religious figure is put in a political setting. The figure, as demonstration of a particular religion in politics, sparked another type of demonstration in the crowd. Pilate's major mistakes began with his assumption that he could reason in that setting with those demonstrators. Yet intentional demonstrations are more for show than for reason. Demonstrators desire to have a point understood, not debated. Speaking as a veteran of demonstrations, I cannot remember a single demonstration whose crowd was open to or desired reason. Demonstrations are valuable only for making a point. Demonstrations are given to excess when asked to do more than they are capable of doing: thinking by numbers. Considering not the religious figure, but the crowd, let us understand political demonstrations to the extent that we can both use them and avoid being used by them.

Are political demonstrations bad? If demonstrations were deemed inherently evil, we would need to ban both the Republican and Democratic Conventions. They are, basically, political demonstrations orchestrated to get points across to the American people. Establishment demonstrations are no less ludicrous than antiestablishment demonstrations are. We can tune in to the next major political party conventions and watch what happens after the words, "I give you the next President of the United States, ______!" Bands play, balloons fall down (or rise up), people dressed in costumes dance, shrill horns shriek, and people parade, carrying signs that show their allegiance. What is the point of all this? They are not there to reason; rather, they are there to motivate themselves and to convince others they are right. If we were to switch channels to the news program, we might see a strikers' picket line outside a factory or a citizens' picket line outside a courthouse. Each is making its point public. When the Constitution of the United States gave us the right of assembly (First Amendment), it was guarding our right to demonstrate.

The good of demonstrations becomes evident when we realize that most people, like Pilate, will not take action on any issue until confronted. Common sense and experience tell us that our involvement increases proportionately to the sense of importance we attach to any issue. Numerous political surveys confirm this link: "Persons are more likely to turn out for elections they perceive to be important."[1] Demonstrations are a way to move a particular issue up the value scale of the intended audience, and a way of provoking response. Would the Vietnam War have ended as quickly without all of the demonstrations that caused political pressure? Probably not. No matter what side of that issue we were on, most would readily admit that the demonstrations were what moved the American people, and eventually the government, to end the war. Would we have the advancements in civil rights today without the demonstrations of the 1960s? Probably not. From the sympathy evoked by pictures of police dogs tearing into peaceful marchers, to the fear evoked by the race riots, our attention was captured. The government was also confronted by those demonstrations, and legislation plus favorable court decisions resulted.

Deliberation after Demonstration. So demonstrations have been and will continue to be valuable. Yet there is a major principle for us all to keep in mind: *Improvements may be made because of demonstrations but are seldom made in the midst of demonstrations.* Jesus withdrew from the crowds for deliberation, but Pilate stood in the midst of the crowd while making his choices. Unlike Pilate, thinking people must distance political decision and action from the emotionalism of the masses. Jesus chose not to add to the fiery atmosphere though he was in the midst of the demonstration. Emotionalism, rather than deliberation, tends to rule at demonstrations. A recent incident in which hundreds of Christians desired to legitimately demonstrate their opposition to a zoning variance illustrates the point.

I sat in a county council's meeting room for a board of adjustments meeting. Although the meetings usually had limited attendance, this night the room was overflowing into the hall. Word had come to the Christians in our area that a new establishment—the "Erotic" something or other—was trying to get a zoning variance. The establishment would not only rent pornographic movies (something that most video clubs in the area were already doing) but would also have "live entertainment." That was new to the area and unwanted by a majority of Christians. Many Christians had come to voice opposition; a few had brought their children.

As the proceedings began, the chairman issued a sensible opening statement to this effect: "I know that many of you are here to voice opposition to this establishment. The board would appreciate it if you would have representative speakers for groups. Please be brief. You will be heard, but when the speeches begin to become repetitive in content, we will end the discussion period to decide the matter." The attorney for the "Erotic" business made his case in a calm and reasoned manner—very polite, very respectable. His point was basically that his client's store would not offer anything that other video stores in the area were not offering except "maybe one or two girls." The obscenity law of the county was new and untested, he implied, and it would be a shame to have to go to court and have it smashed. He was slick. The implication was that an agreeable decision now would save a court battle and a loss of time and revenue.

When he finished, the floor was open for discussion. I was seated (providentially, I think) beside a Christian attorney who was a veteran of many political confrontations in the community at large. He knew I had only lived in the area a year and a half, so he kept me informed privately as the "discussion" progressed publicly.

"Are there any to speak for this business?" the chairman asked. A moment of silence followed as "who would dare?" glances shot around the room. "No one," came the unspoken answer.

"Who will speak against it?" the chairman asked. A gray-haired man in a brown polyester suit raised his hand. "That's one of three political preachers in the area," my attorney guide whispered. "Whenever there is a public forum, a place to be seen and heard on a controversial matter, you usually find them there." The man stood to give a surprisingly brief statement. For a moment I relaxed.

Then I found myself dreading the inevitable: a Christian who would stand and say or do something silly enough to erase the positive impact of the simple presence of two hundred Christian citizens. This happened quickly enough.

A big man walked down to the front of the meeting hall. He was carrying a brown paper bag. *Oh, no,* I thought, *here it comes.*

"That's another one of our political preachers," whispered my guide.

Oh, no, I repeated to myself.

The fellow's face was flushed. He began to speak partly to the board members, partly to the crowd, but mostly to the TV camera. "Do any of you have any idea of the kind of filth we are talking about here? I stopped by a store to buy this pornographic magazine and I just want you to cast your eyes on this smut!" With that he whirled around to flash the pictures to an unready audience. I cannot fully describe the effect on the audience because I could not tell how many were closing their eyes in purity or how many were squinting for better focus. I do know that all felt like they were in a situation out of control. As the demonstrator talked on (most were too shocked to hear what he said), he turned again to show the picture directly into the TV camera. His barrage of "righteous indignation" finally ended. He returned to his seat with his reloaded brown paper bag.

Several more spoke against the zoning variance. A chief of police spoke about the possibilities of increased crime. A counselor spoke about his work with those who had been significantly harmed by their use of pornography. A man stood to give an account of the sexual acts he had seen performed in such an establishment. The discussion grew more consuming. Then, in one final blaze of heat (but not light), a man swaggered to the front. "I am not one of these Christians," he began. "But we all know what kind of vermin go into these places!" "Amen!" came a call from his religious counterpart. "They are not even human," he continued. "Anyone that goes into one of these places is garbage. They are worms, and worse! There is nothing decent about them, and we don't want that human trash around here! They are ______ nothings!"

Something strange happened at this point. It was like a slap in our collective face. Many, I learned afterward, were embarrassed to be linked with that kind of emotional excess and derogatory verbiage. Many of us returned to our cars wishing the point could have been made intelligently, calmly, and with respect for all persons involved. I am not sure that calm, intelligent behavior is possible in a political demonstration that invites all to participate. If it were possible to have demonstrations orchestrated in such a manner, at least two benefits would be ours. First, the increased credibility from those who might oppose us would be remarkable. The tone of voice used by the chairman of that board of adjustments betrayed a combination of condescension and anticipation. He might as well have said, "I know what you are going to say and how you are going to say it before you even begin" to the Christians who had come to demonstrate their concern. What a difference for him it would have made if we had organized to the point where two or three persons could have spoken for us in terms that would challenge his intelligence and sense of values!

Second, orchestrated demonstrations would insure more Christians participating. My wife, who had never been on a picket line in her life, went with me to a one-hour picket line in front of the "Erotic" whatever when it opened in spite of being denied the zoning variance. We did not want to carry a sign, we did not want to chant, we did not want to say clever things to people entering the store. We just wanted to protest what we saw as a violation of community standards and the law. But, midway in the picket time, one of the political preachers brought in a casket with a skeleton in it. The skeleton was named Philip or Phyllis Porno. And when a TV camera arrived (that is the point of a demonstration—to be seen), the cameraman went straight to the casket, and then started filming all of us. Most Christians want to avoid those kinds of tacky tactics. Many who would stand up for their faith intelligently explained will not stand for their faith being so shabbily summarized.

Nevertheless, demonstrations have and will continue to serve a positive purpose. They bring to the attention of all, Christians included, issues that would otherwise be ignored. They prompt people to action. To be ultimately effective, though, we must detach ourselves from them. Unlike Pilate, we must let their value lie solely in the fact that they have captured our attention. Reason based upon the passion of a demonstration usually turns out to be not reason at all, but reaction.

If the demonstration is a group of people instead of a candidate, we can prepare the demonstration stage for purposes of higher thought in several ways. The most effective way is separating the time of the demonstration from the time we make the decision about the issue. Pilate felt hard-pressed for an immediate decision. He may have feared that riot or bad reports to Caesar would result if he did not make a decision immediately. He was provoked to reaction instead of reason. Pilate feared for his safety, his reputation, and his job. Emotional provocation centers the basis for decision making on us, not on the issue at hand. While that is understandable and valid, it is only part of the consideration. Time is needed to quell the inner fears. Surging adrenaline seldom prompts rational questions like, What is best for the common good? or, What is the opposite side to the one being presented by the demonstration? or, What do the emotions in me have to do with the issues at hand?

Separation of confrontation and thinking implies not only time but space. A Christian can avoid Pilate's mistake by postponing a decision and separating physically from the demonstration. Scripture has recorded that every time Pilate had contact with Jesus, he was at the same time, or almost the same time, relating to the Jewish demonstrators. At one point, the demonstrators were not present, so he called them together (Luke 23:13). Such a proximity to the voices calling for a certain action hardly allows for calm reflection on the matter. We have the same tendency as Pilate when we do not consider or research political issues in private but make up our minds while talking to or watching people who are trying to convince us. Whether they are face to face with us, or they are entering our living rooms through the television, we must not be intimidated into a position that is a reaction. We can walk away to think; we can turn off the television to deliberate. That way much of the pressure of the demonstration can fade.

And while we are taking some time in separation from whatever forced our attention to the issue, we can dilute that force by considering alternate opinions. Demonstrations appear to be shouting, "There are only two alternatives in this matter, ours and the one against us. Now decide which side you are on!" There is scriptural evidence that Pilate tried to get creative enough to get around agreeing or disagreeing with the demonstrators. He did come up with the Barabbas alternative so that the demonstrators themselves would relieve him of the decision. His mistake, however, was that he never changed the basic "for or against" mentality. He never stopped to consider the deeper question of truth nor sought out other opinions on the issue of Jesus. He never tested the singular, powerful voice of the demonstration against other voices and opinions which would have created some balance in deliberation. Indeed, it seldom occurs to any of us that we do not have to take a given side in order to take a stand. We are in a position to collect various insights. We are not confined to an ultimatum. Far from adding confusion, taking time to note others' opinions will put our political decisions in a new category. We may be able to add insight instead of only receiving it. And the stand we finally take will be truly ours instead of "theirs." Broadening our basis for decision dilutes not only the pressure to decide; it makes more potent the capacity to decide with accuracy.

Identifying the Issues—In Terms Broader Than Religion

Truth is stranger than fiction; truth is also stronger than friction. It is logical to assume that Christianity is strongest when it is most forceful. It is also logical to assume that if the Christian tradition is under attack, we should fight back. It is almost inconceivable that, at a point where religion is most desperately needed, we would detach ourselves from religious terms. It would be so natural to respond to mockery with a counterattack.

Both Jesus and the religious crowd were threatened. The two reacted differently. The Jews tried to protect their religion by complaining to the authorities. They organized as much political force as they could muster. They mobilized a campaign to save the country, a campaign based on accusation, negativism, and fear. They won the debate, and missed the point.

Jesus, on the other hand, offered no defense. He was not interested in justifying Himself. He was interested in seeking the truth. "For this I have been born, and for this I have come into the world, to bear witness to the truth. Everyone who is of the truth hears my voice" (John 18:37). He used no religious talk. He used the highest universal goal, the truth, and was confident that those seeking the truth would understand Him. Such a strategy made Him vulnerable; such a strategy made Him invincible.

It is sobering today to find Christians choosing the former political strategy instead of the latter. It will cost us more than we realize. If we choose to defend our religion rather than seek the whole truth, we will lose three most important capacities. We will lose our ability to see God outside of our own tradition. We will lose our capacity to influence people, in any positive sense, toward God. We will lose the opportunity to grow in our own faith.

If we are not more interested in truth than in our traditional expressions of religion, we will miss the sovereignty of God. A young lady came into my office recently to ask me questions about our local church. She was trying to decide whether or not to attend. One of the first questions she asked was, "How big a God do you believe in?" I knew what she meant. God is not so small that He resides only in the tradition of my church. And protectionism—aiming to preserve rather than seek—misses what is standing before us. It is like keeping the protective caps on binoculars while we are using them. We can either protect the lenses that were made to see, or we can use them to bring closer what is distant. We cannot do both at once. We cannot see the issues for what they are, nor the candidates for who they are, if we limit our look to our past. God may be doing "a new thing." The question we must ask is, "How could God be involved in this issue or candidate to accomplish His purpose?" Answering that question takes research.

The mandate for this research comes from Jesus. In His trial process He tells the chief priests to look beyond that single glimpse of Him and to search for the whole truth about him: "Why do you question Me? Question those who have heard what I spoke to them" (John 18:21). The statement is an extension of the research process He mentioned previously, recorded in John 5:31-37. The process acknowledges the limitations of a person being his own witness (5:31). The process entails looking to predecessors (5:33) and recent colleagues (18:21). It also advises that we look at one's deeds (5:36) and rely upon the witness of the Spirit. The process is not only a valid guideline for objectively appraising candidates today; it reminds us that as we search for the whole truth about someone, we will be able to see more clearly how God would have us vote. We cannot just listen to a candidate's statements on religious issues and claim to know the candidate adequately. If we can see, additionally, in whose footsteps they follow, and whose company they presently keep, we will get a broader and more comprehensive picture. We can know much about a candidate by knowing the people who would back them politically. It is also crucial to review a record of the person's deeds, both political and personal. Jesus said, "The very works that I do, bear witness of Me." All of a person's works, not just the presence or absence of religious talk, give us a complete picture of him. Certainly it is important to know what he decided on public matters. It is important to note the consistency of those actions. Does the person have a stable and predictable philosophy so that we know, basically, how he or she will vote? Or is the candidate a political opportunist? When we see a record of how a person has reacted to many public issues, we can sense more who that candidate really is and how God might be using him.

The process does not limit us to an examination of public deeds. Jesus included His friends in the "those who have heard what I spoke to them." While there are some things about a candidate's life that should remain private, his or her private life is still an issue. No matter how many times we are told that a candidate's personal life has nothing to do with his political activity, common sense tells us otherwise. Offices do not make laws, people do. We are not depending on offices to govern us with sound judgment, wisdom, and integrity. We are trusting the people we elect to those offices. So we need to know if the person has integrity. A candidate disgraced by his own actions told the American people that he wished everyone could just concentrate on the issues instead of the person. But in the truest sense, the person *is* the issue. He or she is the issue that will determine for us all the other issues. While it is true that a morally good person can make a poor official, we can't expect that the opposite might be true. Is it reasonable to assume that a person with an immoral private life will make moral decisions while in office? Possible, but unlikely.

Narrow religious concerns do not grasp the whole picture. The broader our look, the more we can see of God's potential purpose. Interest in only one area can cause us to ignore much valid information. Studies done over a period of sixteen years found that "the partisan is not really interested in messages from both sides: primarily partisans pick up messages from their own side."[2] But Christ calls us to learn the whole truth before deciding what God is doing.

The strategy of defending a religious tradition also eliminates our capacity to positively influence other people toward God. When we are so narrowly focused upon our own concerns, we cannot expect others to really hear us. The religious crowd that presented their concerns to Pilate was clearly purposed in defending their religion and political advantage. The charges they presented were significant crimes. Not only did they charge that He was misleading the nation, but that He was also "forbidding to pay taxes to Caesar, and saying that He Himself is . . . a King" (Luke 23:2). Pilate did not investigate; he hardly heard. Instead, he promptly declared, "I find no guilt in this man" (Luke 23:4). How could he decide so fast? Pilate reacted not to their statements but to their motivation. Pilate could see that their motivation was envy (Matt. 27:18). He had no trouble perceiving that their political ends were focused upon their own benefit. He had no desire to help them or join them in their goals.

Christians defending a religious tradition are similarly dismissed. And why shouldn't we be? The world does not give a hoot about our religion, nor will they until they perceive that we care more about the world than our own interests. If evangelicals in politics cause people to dismiss Christianity because of our defense of it, how tragic that is!

We are called to be witnesses (Acts 1:8), to point beyond ourselves. Christ shows us two important prerequisites to witnessing. First, we need to get rid of the counterattack mentality. Counterattack not only kills our own search for truth, it kills everyone else's as well. Jesus quietly and calmly told the truth when under fire. The truth was His strength. He did not need any other justification. "But Jesus made no further answer; so that Pilate was amazed" (Mark 15:5). In contrast, counterattack simply solidifies separate positions, and no positive influence can stem from it. Though there was no evident influence in His trial process, Jesus never switched strategies. His attitude never hardened, and it kept no one who was interested away.

The second prerequisite Jesus modeled was His use of

nonreligious language. Religious terms can build walls, so rather than state our concerns in terms everyone can know and understand, we punctuate our lingo with "Christianese." We assume that using Scripture to back up our points, or shouting "Amen!" to a speech will communicate something of the Spirit to people. It does communicate a spirit—a spirit of self-centered arrogance. Jesus realized the vast difference between the spiritual world and the earthly world (John 18:36). Because of that realization, He used a concept that is universally understood and attractive: truth.

The search for truth in any issue or candidate puts religious and nonreligious on common ground. As any Christian who is honest with himself knows, the revealed truth of Scripture does not automatically transfer onto the contemporary issues of our nation. It does not replace the gathering of facts. It does not save us from the need to calculate the consequences of our vote. Nor does Scripture relieve us from the need to draw truth from those outside our religion. The search for truth is hampered by any special lingo that would make communication undesirable or more difficult. Any statement we make that sounds religiously esoteric creates walls.

A real test of Christianity in politics is this: Can everyone see his own benefit in our political stance, even if he is not of our faith? Religious language and religious ambition will turn people off; they will shut down the search. Both the crowd, who thought they had enough truth, and Pilate, who was too preoccupied with noisy religionists, could not get interested in looking for truth that day. But it is not always so. When people are detached from the demonstration, they would rather know the truth than not. The people who work to see that *everyone* wins in their political stance, and who talk in terms that communicate to everyone, will follow in the footsteps of Christ.

Language is important, as is our desire for wisdom, in our third concern: that we not be blocked from growing in our faith. Language does not just describe reality, it molds our perception of reality. To limit ourselves to religious language in describing political problems is to limit our ability to conceptualize those problems. Religious language so necessary in describing the "other realm" (spiritual concerns) may not exactly fit "this realm." Therefore we could miss much, not just in relation to other people but in relation to our own understanding, if compelled to stick with religious terms for political analysis.

Even more important is our attitude of openness. The person not of our faith could very well be a friend. Those who threaten us religious folk can probably teach us more about completing our own faith than we realize. So it was with Jesus and the Jews; so it is with our "opposition" and us. The question an "opposition" person poses to us is not whether or not we are wrong. The real question posed is whether or not our understanding of the truth is large enough to include the opposition's point. If our understanding is too small, we need to increase it for the good of the faith. If people raise issues directly challenging our religion, ones that we cannot answer to the satisfaction of believer and nonbeliever alike, we need to take a significant step of growth. Why should we feel threatened if we only seek the truth?

In fact, truth will fulfill the Scripture and outlast any political battle. God points us to the truth. If we choose to respond to political issues as a challenge to grow into that area of truth, if we see political issues as opportunities to learn from others of different perspectives, we have no cause for defensiveness.

We will get stronger as the battle wears on, not more drained. He will expand our spirit, our influence, and our intellect. We will be able to examine God's whole truth, and He will add immeasurably to the faith in Him that we have now.

Identifying the Issues—In Terms Deeper Than Politics

The religious crowd missed the truth because they were too focused on religion. Pilate missed it because he was too focused on politics. Defining issues and candidates in terms broader than religion will help us in searching for the truth for all. Thinking through issues and candidate's strategies in ways deeper than politics will always help us in searching for truth.

Politics is the art of fixing conflict. It can be more than that, but it seldom is. Pilate typified the temptation to temporarily quell a disturbance rather than make a decision that would stand the test of time. Pilate thought of a quick solution, not a principle. He thought in terms of relief, not cure.

The great strength Christians should be able to bring to the American political process is one of depth. Those who see the world in more than one dimension, who think in ages longer than this life, can be an invaluable voice calling for depth in decision making. The basis of our decision to follow Christ was that we would live in light of the future. That basis is also best for politics and quite rare in politics. Politics, as Pilate knew, gets so complicated that the attention shifts to the process rather than the results. Politics is compromise. Politics is swapping favors. At times the process involves the very real ultimatum, "You can do what you know to be right, or you can secure your own political future." The threat in John 19:12 reflects this practical versus principle battle. The crowd threatens Pilate by saying, "If you release this man, you are no friend of Caesar." He was hearing that his political life was at stake. We need not be too critical when we read the next verse: "When Pilate heard these words, he brought Jesus out." Political officeholders, unlike many of their constituents, put their reputations (and hence their jobs) on the line with their votes. It is far from being in an easy position. The alternatives sometimes seem to be that they either do what will keep them in office or they play the role of martyr, dying a political death for a good cause.

There is no better example of this dilemma right now than the phenomenon of our national debt. How we got to this place, this financial black hole, is a matter of complex history and great partisan debate. But the emergency nature of the problem is becoming quite apparent to everyone. Without naming the figures (they are increasing at a rate so fast that they would be obsolete before the chapter was complete), we are all aware that the interest payment alone on the debt has the power to bring down our national economy in several ways. We are also aware that the borrowing-against-our-future mentality has become as much of a handicap as the debt itself. Individual consumer debt is following the example of the government (or vice versa). And, finally, we are aware of the current cause of the debt's increase: the government, feeling pressure from us constituents desiring more goodies, will not discipline itself to spend less. We all know the cure. It entails getting less from the government, doing without many current benefits. Our Congress knows that, too. But Congress faces incredible pressure, politically life-threatening, to sacrifice only the benefits that will bring the least cry from the crowd. Those are few and far between, if they exist at all.

We are being killed by our weakness for stopgap measures and temporary fixes. We are engaged in convenience thinking rather than consequential thinking. We also do not seem to realize that every action we take is a precedent, a desensitization for a like action in the near future. And we have forgotten the fact that principals in government can choose principled ways as well as practical ways. Let us take a deeper look into each of these areas.

The convenience-versus-consequences thinking sounds like a neat cliche from a flippant sermon. It is actually a form of immaturity that has dire side effects. In the beginning of our country's history, our leaders were aware that we were an "experiment." We were not sure whether or not we had much of a future, so in the decision making we took much care to consider the consequences. The population at large did not demand convenience, nor did they reflexively link government with their personal problems. Life was a struggle, and everyone knew it. The survival of the country was part of the population's concern. We have, of course, "progressed." Since the industrial revolution enabled us to think of jelly as well as bread, and since World War II gave us not just confidence of survival but arrogance as a developing superpower, the country's survival seldom enters our minds. As personal and national survival ceased to be an issue, convenience took its place. With the help of modern technology, convenience has almost obliterated the notion of consequence. We can have sex without pregnancy and sweetness without sugar, and now the Food and Drug Administration is reviewing a product that would eliminate calories and cholesterol from such delectables as pie, ice cream, and chocolate. We now have the option of developing the attitude of "all things being equal, I'd rather have whatever makes my life easier and more fun." The only time this attitude may be suspended is when group survival is again the issue. During those times the concern for individual convenience can change to a concern about the consequences of one's actions on the group. Pilate saw his decision in terms of his own convenience, in terms of his own political life. He did not consider that, if the claims of Christ were true in a deeper sense, the consequences of his action meant his spiritual condemnation. Was Jesus really on trial that day? Hardly. Pilate was. The followers of Christ can continue to call our own attention, as well as the attention of our governing officials and fellow citizens, to the consequences of our convenience. We are on trial. Every decision that relieves us of a burden has a price. Consequential thinking is done with the attitude, "I must find out the ultimate cost of this decision. It looks as if others will have to pay the full price. But there probably is a hidden cost for me or this nation. What is it? Am I willing to pay it?"

Identifying issues in terms deeper than politics also means coming to grips with this fact: each action we take sets a precedent. Our entire justice system judges primarily on the basis of legal precedents. We realize that. But when we vote for candidates or consider an issue, we somehow see it as an isolated event. There is no validity to such an assumption. The strategies of successful candidates or the legislative issues seem to us to be very changeable. We tend to think, "We'll see if this works. If it doesn't, we'll change." But the trend a candidate sets, or the mark a piece of legislation makes on our direction, is indelible. Once we take action, even though we realize later that action may have been unwise, it is easier for us to take it again. How many times did Pilate go back to the crowd to make a decision, even though he knew they had not come to the right decision previously? Three times he knowingly made the same mistake. Every act taken, indeed every option considered, becomes a precedent for its twin in the near future. It is entirely appropriate then to ask whether a candidate or an issue would be one we would want to keep long term.

Finally, principals can create principles as well as practicality. Principles are long-lasting, all-encompassing, statements of truth. The chief example of this kind of thinking is our Constitution. Yes, we know it is not perfect. In its bicentennial year Justice Thurgood Marshall had outspoken criticism of it and its authors. Justice Warren Burger replied, "Every document except perhaps the Ten Commandments has its flaws." The Constitution, however, was and is a work of art that combines the practicality of politics with the enduring wisdom of principles. It was concerned with the larger and deeper issues of forming a more perfect union, establishing justice, securing the blessing of liberty. It was concerned with the practical aspects of insuring domestic tranquility, providing for the common defense, and promoting the general welfare. It seems that we spend more time making political decisions on the basis of immediate tranquility, or on defense versus welfare, than we do on forming a more perfect union with justice. We have made politics too practical, too shallow, too temporarily defined.

The principals (we, the people), through questions we ask ourselves and our representatives, can look into what principle is represented in political action. If Pilate is insuring "domestic tranquility," how is that balanced with justice or welfare? Those who follow Christ can be much-needed reminders that principles should guide practicality, not the other way around. On the major issues we need to ask our representatives what principles are guiding specific decisions. Officeholders are special people and need special attention. As in any job, the daily routine can confine one's concern to what works, and principles can be forgotten. Reminders are in order, and Christians who live their lives based on deeper than surface concerns are the part of "We, the people" who will ask those important questions.

Too much religious activity toward government is antagonistic. Christian interest groups are too often like all others. But the Christlike may want to do as Jesus did and bring up the deeper-than-action side of the issue to our officials. We may want to write them and ask, What are the long-lasting principles by which you have taken action on ____________? Are there any moral or religious principles involved as you see it? What do you hope it will resolve years from now? Can you point to the truth of the matter for me? We might cause some reflection that will do us all good.

Notes

1. Lester W. Milbrath and M. I. Goel, *Political Participation: How and Why Do People Get Involved in Politics?* (Chicago: Rand McNally, 1977), 40.
2. Ibid.

EIGHT

The Pilate Program, Part 2: Assuming Responsibility

Be to the world a sign that, while we as Christians do not have all the answers, we do know and care about the questions.

Billy Graham

Let's be honest: for most of us politics is either confusing, boring, or futile. Oh, it is not terribly difficult to fulfill the first of the demands of our citizenship: awareness. Television news, C-Span, daily newspapers, and news magazines can each be the demonstration that confronts us with issues. If we are very fortunate, our local church may even provide information about politicoreligious issues. And the first three steps of the Pilate Program do not require Herculean effort. We would willingly detach the demonstration and examine the issues with more breadth than one religious tradition and more depth than what is politically expedient. That is, we would examine them if we had the time, or if we were in the right mood, or if we were forced by emergency.

Awareness of the issues gives us the ability to respond, but we need more. The difference between *response ability* and *responsibility* is roughly that of putting an "i" in the gap. Most people drop out at this point. Pilate did.

Pilate, like many people, used the political process to hide. He rationalized that his anonymity might help achieve unanimity, which was better for the country. It all worked out very nicely for Pilate, as it does for us. If the issue turned out well, he could reap the benefits. If the issue turned out badly, he could not be blamed. So Pilate claimed, "I am innocent . . . see to that yourselves" (Matt. 27:24). Then he disappeared into neutrality.

Like Pilate, many of us have legitimate, even powerful, reasons for not taking action on what we know. Our reluctance may stem from our lack of definite solutions. And the issues *are* complicated. Pilate's job was not only to think about justice, but to maintain peace. In the case of Jesus, two good political goals were conflicting. We, too, face those complicated, no-easy-answer issues. We desire to help the helpless of our nation without accommodating freeloaders. Yet it is difficult to set up a freeloader detector that does not destroy families by requiring a no-father household. We desire a strong national defense, but we want to avoid a militant mentality that will send our children into unnecessary combat (or nuclear holocaust). We desire to have the government provide necessary services, but we see a mounting national debt that not only threatens economic collapse but also reflects our national tendency not to delay gratification. Few of us feel qualified to define "necessary services" for all, and none of us feel a definition is coming fast enough from our political leaders. How does one respond to such a complex situation? Most would say, "I don't know. You decide," and drop out of the conversation.

If we cannot solve the political problems, which have secondary moral implications, perhaps we would fare better in the religiopolitical issues, which have primarily moral implications. We desire to save the unborn, stop the godlessness in the public schools, and preserve the values foundational to our life together as a nation—all while not imposing our religion on others. We are against the exploitation of people by pornography, while also being against trends of government censorship. Simply put, every major issue is complicated. It is no wonder we leave the answers to the crowd. The answers may be up to us, but they are beyond us—so we quit.

Then we find out what Pilate found out—others have even worse answers.

The transition from awareness to personal, responsible participation is difficult. Most of us are not only not inclined in that direction, we will do whatever is convenient to avoid it. We are not a society where the traditional means of political motivation work anymore. We are not moved by duty, nor by guilt, nor by the gradual deterioration of society. The American Christian can be motivated to act politically in brief intervals by crisis or scandal. But after a brief period of personal, responsible participation, we sink back into the crowd.

One transition from awareness to participation will work: prayer.

Deciding Inside

Most of us begin with three major obstacles when considering political involvement. First, we wonder what it will profit us in relation to what it will cost us. Second, we wonder how much or how little responsibility is really "mine." Third, we wonder what the correct answers are to the really complex issues. Only prayer can resolve all three obstacles.

God Transforms the I. When we ask first what we will profit, we must realize the I that perverts and ruins all is the author of the question, and that I must go. The I, the Ego described in chapter 5, is hungry for power, domination, and self-protection. That I will pervert any instrument for justice into one for personal advantage. That I will use any power it has for escape or lordship, whichever is the most self-serving course. That I was Pilate, and that I can be the American Christian who will not carry out any political decision or area of work in a way that will benefit others over self. "Well," some will say, "that is the American system. The Founding Fathers planned for such selfish goals. That is why we have a system of checks and balances. People will be people; the horribly selfish I will always be seen at the center of political efforts." That sounds like profound realism; it is rot.

Christians, take warning. Although the American system is realistic in supposing that properly checked power groups will be the norm in our country, we are not called to be one of them. Being a special interest group is not necessarily synonymous with being a self-centered interest group. Special could really mean special in terms of character as well as concern. The cancerous I can be transformed by direct conversation with God. The cost of transformation is submission. No direction will be given, no difference in politics will be seen, if we go to God attempting to manipulate Him toward our answer. Asking the rhetorical, What is truth? and then turning away to do what we would have done anyway is a contradiction. It results in the nonbelievers' cynical viewing of "Christian" participation. It results also in despotism disguised as religion in Christians.

For many, it is very difficult to believe the malignant I that seeks supremacy can be transformed into the servant *i* that would actually take personal responsibility for the benefit of *all* people. It is difficult to fathom that prayer would change the I to *expect* the cost to exceed the political benefit, as part of what we gladly give in obedience. Yet it is not only possible, it is God's hallmark for those who listen.

God Assigns the Specifics. Like Pilate, Christians tend toward an "all or nothing" approach to politics. Many do not want to get involved because they believe they could easily become consumed with all of the problems. Yet prayer will also result in defined assignments and boundaries.

"The people" do have a huge responsibility. Like the general stewardship command of Genesis 1:28, commanding people to "rule over . . . the earth," an individual has a scope of responsibility much larger than any individual's ability. That is why God instituted government and why we only have a part. For what part, and how large a part, we must progress to Genesis 2:15. In that passage God gives a specific call to a specific person for a specific area of responsibility: "Then the Lord God took the man and put him into the garden of Eden to cultivate it and keep it." God outlines our particular work and includes some areas of political responsibilities.

We can recognize the specific issues or candidates we may be called to attend to by the burden we have for them in prayer or the harvest we have seen from them. The proportion of our work—the space we devote to politics, family, business, church—will vary from person to person and even from season to season. But it will be from God, received in direct conversation with Him.

In the midst of prayer, we will know two things that will make an immense difference in our action. We will know that God has a plan for our lives. We will also know that our action is not something we are doing for Him but something we are doing *from* Him. Of course, all prayer should be confirmed by Scripture and wise Christian counsel. But God's direct assignment is a relief from the feeling, "I have to do it all." His assignment is also a commissioning to do what will make the greatest contribution to His world.

God Directs the Decisions. We want answers. And we want to make sure our answers are correct. Like Pilate, we find it easier to hear the answers of the crowd than to receive the answers from God. Yet prayer that has been informed by both the newspaper and the Bible is the Christian's way to the correct inner decision. Any other method tends to produce the crowd's decision in disguise. God desires that individuals follow Him and no other (Exod. 20:3). That is not easy, but voting booths and prayer closets have much in common.

Voting booths are made for one person. Many of us can remember the first time we stepped inside a voting booth. Voting seemed like such an awesome responsibility to me that I felt less than adequate to make up my mind. Maybe, if I could have taken a group of people into the booth, we together could have made a wiser choice than I alone. There were so many names I did not recognize. There were issues numbered and levered, issues to which I had given little thought. I felt the need for a group of people to give me assurances about my choices. But the rules were clear—one person to a booth.

There is a public-private conflict inherent in the structure of American politics. The political ideal calls individuals to make decisions for the good of the whole group. Political strategy tries to persuade individuals to make those decisions on the basis of loyalty to a particular subgroup's interests. One requires the person to act as an individual; the other influences him not to think as an individual.

Group thinking is as attractive to many individuals as it is to political strategists. Group thinking can eliminate the uncomfortable process of individual contemplation and prayer. It can also eliminate the threat of ostracism. In 1956 I remember watching television with my grandfather. A program having to do with the presidential election prompted me to announce to my grandfather that I was old enough to have a political opinion. "If I could vote," I said confidently, "I'd be for Ike." My grandfather flinched. "Oh, no, Joey," he said in a tone filled with pain for not having taught me better. "You *couldn't* do that!" "Why not?" I asked, expecting to hear some dastardly news about Ike. My grandfather replied, "Because he's a Republican and we are Democrats!" Class dismissed.

Group-based voting has a strong, if deteriorating, history in our country. More specifically, religious group-based voting has a stronger precedent than most of us have been taught. In the beginning days of our country, it would have been no surprise to find people voting on the basis of their religious group given the intense sectarianism of the earliest communities. But also from the mid-nineteenth century to the present, religious group-based voting has been found to be a factor. Robert Booth Fowler has recorded what historians have found:

> Religious divisions, often inseparably tied to ethnic differences, drew the political lines on the American map. The divisions were principally between pietists vs. nonpietists (or ritualists). Pietists included Methodists, Baptists (if not Southern), and less liturgical Lutherans. They were almost

> overwhelmingly Republican regardless of where they lived. . . . On the other hand, Roman Catholics, liturgical Lutherans, and most Germans (Lutheran, Reformed, Catholic, but not pietist) stood on the other side and were usually Democrats. . . . Pietists were frankly moralistic in their understanding of religion. They saw themselves led to reform people and America and they rarely had much hesitation in proposing to use the State, its laws and policies, to accomplish their ends. Nonpietists, on the other hand, tended to emphasize church rituals and sacraments as more important to their conception of religion than moral crusades. They also had a notable easygoing (in comparison with pietists) attitude about human behavior and consistently proved more tolerant and less interested in government regulation of personal behavior . . . a good deal of the politics of the second half of the nineteenth century encouraged as well as reflected religious-ethnic divisions in the country. Especially as the decades went by and the pietists more and more felt threatened.[1]

While it is difficult to discern how much religious group-based voting is based on religion rather than other factors, it is not difficult to assume the importance of religion as a source of voter identity. We may also assume that individuals still desire to go along with a larger group when deciding on religious issues. So voting on the basis of one's religious group has both a history and a current attraction, especially in the pietist camp. While public opinion polls in this century suggest that before the 1970s religion was not a major factor at the polls (with the exception of the Roman Catholic candidates for president, Smith in 1928 and Kennedy in 1960), things are changing. Robert Booth Fowler observes, "Abortion, prayer in public schools, the Moral Majority, nuclear weapons, and so much else on the political agenda are linked with assorted religious groups and conflicts. Religion is very much back in politics . . . we may indeed see a sharp rise in religious voting. Its form will be different, but its impact could be substantial."[2] It will be interesting to note what form religious group decision making toward voting will take. The Pilate Program would question the value of group decision making, even the group that is a religious one. It is plainly inferior to individual decisions based on prayer.

Both Pilate and the religious crowd made their decisions about Jesus on the basis of their group identity. It was not just the fact that they were caught up in a demonstration. Nor was their missing the truth only due to their not being open to all the facts. They had the wrong guides. The religious crowd listened solely to their religious leaders. "The chief priests and the elders persuaded the multitudes to ask for Barabbas, and to put Jesus to death" (Matt. 27:20). The pressure to conform to a predetermined political decision was substantial for the individuals involved. And Pilate was not much more free from his own group identity. He was, foremost in his own mind, the representative of the Roman Empire. As an individual he had a decision to make. He could have made it on the basis of his closeness to Jesus, but he was a member of the ruling party. History had dealt him a most important hand, but at the mere mention of Caesar he folded.

Politics is essentially a group activity. But, as with religion, it must primarily be an individual decision. Jesus modeled isolation for deliberation and resolve, just as He modeled group involvement for ministry. Repeatedly in the Gospels we see the pressured Jesus alone, in deepest thought and prayer. Just before being brought to trial, Jesus was alone in Gethsemane finding direction to face the political conflict (Luke 22:39-44). If we think about it, isolation is the appropriate place to get guidance for our political decisions as well as our religious ones.

When we are alone, the issue has time to sink down to our insides. It becomes a supreme matter for our attention. In a conversation with other people the issue may be bantered too lightly; in a conversation with God it is given the gravity it deserves. In public we are hurried to a "yea" or "nay." In private the question, What shall I do with [this candidate or issue]? has time to sink way down to where the Holy Spirit dwells. We can trust the Holy Spirit to guide us. He will bring to our minds what Christ has said (John 14:26) and all that Christ is now saying (John 16:14,15). He will speak in our hearts where Scripture is hidden (Ps. 119:11) and where it is available to apply. He will guide us into all the truth (John 16:13).

We cannot emphasize strongly enough how difficult it is for anyone to separate his decision making from that of his local church or other influence groups. Individual prayer is work. Arranging consistent times of prayer is labor. It is a real commitment for a Christian to get alone with God when it is time to pray about political decisions. But deciding inside is a commitment to trust God, not our influence group, to guide us into political truth. Whether God leads all praying Christians to vote the same is not the point. Developing trust, and the hearing of God, is the point. One truth stands self-evident: the unity we seek will certainly never come from politics or human agreement. If it is unity for which we hope, our only hope is in the Holy Spirit. God does not speak with a forked tongue. Eventually we will all hear the same thing from Him. But first we must train ourselves to listen to Him. To let Him be our guide in personal decisions about politics, as well as all else, is the difficult but ultimate commitment.

From Prayer to Action

If we have a direct leading in prayer and we do not take action, then we are fools or traitors or cowards. We do not need to be superspiritual to be led by God. No scriptural record shows that Pilate ever prayed, yet he had a clear inkling about the innocence of Jesus. The Gospel of John records that no less than three times did Pilate voice this feeling that Jesus had "no guilt" (John 18:38; 19:4, 6). If skeptical Pilate could have an inkling, cannot Christians expect the inner leading of God? Pilate took the inner leading to be nonbinding when it came time to put it into action. "Pilate made efforts to release Him. . . . He then delivered Him up to them to be crucified"

(John 19:12, 16). On the other hand, when Jesus walked out of the garden from prayer, no person nor circumstance could keep him from obeying the inner decision. When Peter drew his sword to defend Jesus from the results determined in prayer, Jesus asked the question for us all, "The cup which the Father has given Me, shall I not drink it?" (John 18:11). The inner voice is not a feeling, it is a command. It would be wise to consider God's commands and five basic actions He may give to us.

Action Perfects

Action perfects our faith, our witness, and our world. James 2:22 says, "As a result of the works, faith was perfected." The Greek word for perfected means "brought to its proper fulfillment" or "completed in its appropriate use." God is interested in developing in us all a faith perfected by works. He wants our faith to grow by what we do. He does not just desire our behavior to change (the focused interest of politics), He desires that our faith be increased by our acting upon it. The health of our faith is determined by exercising it. Faith not dear enough to stimulate action is dead.

Action also perfects our witness. Not only is God waiting for us to participate politically, the world is, too. Do we mean what we believe? How will the world know if we do not act upon it? Let's not be intimidated by secular people who disparage Christian involvement in politics. It is not the Christian involvement but usually the manner and the tone of Christian involvement that bothers them. Nonbelievers watch to see whether the followers of Christ will ever make a significant difference outside the walls of their churches. Recently an article in our local newspaper explained that the school board would be reviewing sex education curriculum. The paper quoted the chairperson as saying, "I hope we can get the committee organized before all the Christians start talking about morals and abstinence." That sounds like a derisive remark, and I am sure it was meant that way. Yet it is also a remark that connotes a certain respect. She was viewing the participation of Christians as certain enough and significant enough to concern her. I wonder how much her respect for Christianity would decrease if we were not interested or strong enough to give input. Our involvement is not only to do and say "what we are supposed to," it is also to give others grounds to take Christianity seriously. When Christ becomes a force to be reckoned with, he will also become a face to be recognized.

As for action perfecting the world, perhaps "perfecting" is too strong a word. Maybe "limiting destruction" would be more accurate. Whatever phrase is on our minds, the point is that God loves people. He loves us enough that He does not exclude government as a tool by which He can inspire us to help each other. Through our government we have the chance to influence profoundly the lives of people all over the world. No, we cannot convert them through government. Yes, their eternal salvation is most important. But that does not mean that every other provision that could be made through government is unimportant. It does not mean that the stewardship of the earth is not a concern because conversion is. Our government has certain powers, minor next to God's, but still rather potent. Our government can feed the hungry, relieve people from oppression, even model strength with integrity to the world. But without action from the Christ-followers in our nation, much of that potential will be left incomplete, unfulfilled.

Some Basic Actions

God will call some people to unique service in government. He has done that historically with kings such as David, vice-pharaohs such as Joseph, judges such as Samson and Deborah, queens such as Esther, and prophets such as Nathan. But how many Davids or Josephs or Nathans does God need? If He is not calling us to be the leading government official, what, then, will He call most of us to do?

1. Read regularly and converse. That sounds so common, but it is not. Most of us can count on one hand the number of

deeply committed Christians we know who can tell what a pork barrel rider is—or cares. There are so few disciples who can discern intelligently and with gentle spirit the most basic contemporary political issues. There are even fewer who have prayed about them and been able to find a scriptural context that speaks to the principle.

Reading and conversation are works that follow from prayer and continually add to prayer. Prayer stimulates the research; research sharpens the prayer inquiry. The Holy Spirit can use political material to move us to take appropriate action. It is not unlike how He uses Scripture.

The source of the reading material is somewhat important. Many evangelicals use materials that come from a clearly evangelical slant. That is fine. The liberal Christian perspective and the humanist perspective are also valuable. The newspaper usually has a section for political news (the bias varies with the paper). Some papers have summaries of how your government representatives voted that week. Particular sources will be listed later, but the reason broad scope is important is plain: when we read from more than one perspective, we can be more sure that the Holy Spirit is forming our opinion, rather than the writers of our source material. Though the Holy Spirit will lead us to truth in any source, it is helpful to read with God's overview rather than someone's warmed-over sermonic perspective.

2. Write. Everything we have always wanted to say to the government through our congressman is on the end of our pen. Everything we want to say to our community through a letter to the editor is on the end of our pen. What we may desire to say to our school board or county commissioner simply needs an envelope and a stamp. The dominion of the world started with a seed cultivated; the opinion of our government can also start at the seed level.

It may be rather intimidating for those who have never written before to do so. Several lists of "how to" write our congressmen net the following commonsense points:

a. Spell his whole name correctly—*The Hon.* ___________ on the envelope and *Dear Mr.* __________ on the letter.
b. Keep your letter brief and write legibly.
c. Know your subject, including the numbers of any bills to which you are referring.
d. Be specific in stating your opinion or desire.
e. Don't threaten.
f. Make sure the matter is a federal one.

Items *a–e* would apply in writing other officials. When writing to any forum, newspaper, school board, or government official, be sure to link your concern to the general public well-being.

Also remember, public officials will be limited severely if the only word they hear from their constituency is a positive or negative vote. Our government policies will be limited to the perspective of our representatives if citizens do not express ideas as well as verdicts. Civil service, like any vocation, has its own parochial pattern of thinking. Conversations with other civil servants can net some new ideas and solutions, but not very different perspectives. Without the expression of ideas, questions, and problems from the citizens, a representative type of government can become every bit as isolated as a dictatorship. The isolation of our governing officials is not intentional, but it is very real.

More specifically, Christians need to write public officials about particular politicoreligious matters that concern us all. Where will these representatives find informed, spiritual input if not from us? We cannot expect nonbelievers to make godly decisions in a vacuum. Neither can we expect believing representatives to enact such decisions without our support. Civil servants need new, fresh, workable, and, yes, *godly* input. They also might be delighted to hear that we are praying for them. Unfortunately, most of our government representatives have an image of Christians who are more ready to cut them off at the knees than to spend time on our knees for them.

3. Vote.

4. Do volunteer work in politics. Some will be called to more service than insight. If our prayer closet generates enthusiasm or burdens but no verbally expressible input, perhaps the Lord will call us to serve. There are some who are naturals for service. Martha personalities (as Martha is described in Luke 10:38-42) are task- and activity-oriented. This is also true of people who have the spiritual gifts of helps or service. When some issue or candidate comes the way of these people, the response is to *do* something about it. More accurately, it is to do many things about it. These types of folks may take their God-given predisposition and leading to be an invaluable support to a political campaign or issue.

Some "Marthas" will be fascinated by the activity of politics and choose to be a mainstay of the community in political activities. Such people, if they keep their balance in ministering to their family as well as their work, are continual witnesses to God's quiet corps. These folks have a serving ministry that sets others free to proclaim and explain (Acts 6:2-4). "Marthas" are terrific in doing necessary precinct work such as mailings, phone calling, registering people to vote, working at the polls, etc. They are the organizers of political conventions. These men and women put forth the 90 percent effort it takes to attract voters (the other 10 percent being the "glory jobs").

Some "Marthas" will be called to one particular issue, or perhaps a few, for a limited period of time. They may have a special "burden" for issues concerning children, or women, or civil rights. Such a ministry is also valuable to model that short-term callings are as valid to God as lifelong volunteer careers. If our ideal is obedience, not simple human effort, then the Lord is in charge of the length of service. Many times He will use volunteer public service as a transition into another ministry.

5. God may lead you to run for office. Politics is as honorable work for God as any other. An evangelical in political office can be a powerful witness. With the single exception of celebrity religious leaders and the complications they would

bring, evangelical officeholders can be most powerful as they live their normal Christian lives without special crusades. For example, Mark Hatfield, United States senator from Oregon, has had a tremendous impact on the political scene. His stands on the issues do not always match the typical evangelical agenda, but his faith is the guiding principle in all of his life. He understands that serving the Lord will at times lead him into conflict with the culture and with government, but political office is his calling. Hatfield's presence in politics points to the sometimes overlooked power of an individual who goes about his daily life as a Christian. He witnesses verbally when the Lord gives him an opening, but his mission is not to evangelize Congress. Hence, his potential to evangelize, not as a puppet for religious groups but as a deeply devoted individual, increases as the years go by. As with all vocations, individual example does more to penetrate American pluralism than does organized religious group effort. Organized religious group effort may overcome pluralism in power, but it does more to irritate and arouse suspicions than draw people to the Lord.

Perhaps God is calling you as an individual to be a part of His work in politics. It is not a more holy calling than being a Christian ditch-digger and no less holy a calling than being a nationally recognized evangelist. It is simply a job for which God may have made you. If so, He will whisper it in the prayer closet.

Pilate, like many of us, never really took action. He went through the normal political motions. He had some inner leading, but it did not lead him. He dispensed with his political duty as painlessly as possible, doing what seemed at the time to serve the best interests of all, except Jesus.

Imitators of Christ in politics will do directly the opposite. If we are confronted with a political issue that grabs us religiously, and most of us will be if we simply read the newspaper long enough, we are not to be in motion. We are to be in prayer. As with Christ, any action we take must arise from prayer. As with Christ, the action will not aim primarily at expanded worldly power or visible results. The action will be simple obedience.

If all political action we take is a result of prayer, our actions will have a very different tone from other political actions. That action (participation) will be filled with tolerance and healing, rather than competition.

A Healing Presence in Politics

There are two types of tolerance. One type of tolerance ennobles; the other type of tolerance corrupts. One type of tolerance is active; the other type of tolerance is passive. The first type of tolerance is not afraid of nor destroyed by conflict. The second type is many times the excuse for avoiding conflict at all costs. The first tolerance is necessary to the extension of ideals and beliefs; the second arrests ideals and beliefs for disturbing the peace.

Americans and Christians have defined tolerance inaccurately. Much of what has passed for tolerance in this country has been indifference or empty-headedness. True tolerance comes in the midst of conflict. True tolerance respects and sharpens; it does not dull or ignore. True tolerance has a power to cultivate the hallmarks of both discipleship and patriotism—passion and freedom. But before we exercise true tolerance, we need to exorcise false tolerance.

Tolerance is not indifference. One is a virtue of hard work; the other is a sin of laziness. Both the nation and the Lord require of us maximum effort to effect our destiny. On the experiential level, individual participation is demanded. Passion is required. Arthur Schlesinger, Jr., writes, "Americans can take pride in their nation, not as they claim a commission from God and a sacred destiny, but as they fulfill their deepest values in an enigmatic world. America remains an experiment. Only hard work at the experiment will achieve the destiny. The outcome is by no means certain."[3] Scripture calls for the same passion in our efforts. Christ chides the people of Laodicea when He says, "I know your deeds, that you are neither cold nor hot; I would that you were cold or hot. So because you are lukewarm, and neither hot nor cold, I will spit you out of My mouth" (Rev. 3:15-16).

Indifference that tries to pass as tolerance is not acceptable. We cannot hang our acceptance of other people's opinions over shrugged shoulders. The cultural admiration for "cool" elevates aloof attitudes. It dissuades us from emotional investment in participation. It also encourages retreat from any action met with opposition. We assume dignity depends upon either agreement or isolation. We cannot picture dignity as growing stronger in the midst of disdain.

No, true tolerance requires caring and participation with the opposition. It involves healing by hearing without retreat. It involves healing by offering our side without apology, whatever the reaction. True tolerance is emotional work.

Tolerance is not empty-headedness. Many acquire false tolerance by suspending judgment. To be able to accept another's opinion we simply say, "I just won't think about it." Or, even worse, Americans (including Christians) tend to minimize differences by saying, "Oh, it's all the same. Any theory of government will get us to approximately the same place. We are all just people, and any opinion that a person sincerely holds is pretty much as good as any other." Thus we maximize false tolerance by minimizing intellectual discernment. It is essentially agreement by stupor.

In fact, there are critical differences in various forms of government and religion. In fact, if one cannot rate relative values of these forms for the sake of tolerance, that person is crippled intellectually to the point of being dangerous. We can certainly see the necessity to emphasize the value of *people* who hold different beliefs than we do. That is what TV shows like "Phil Donahue in Russia" or the various exchange programs of our schools attempt to do. But in presenting the value of people, they gloss over philosophical time bombs. Our television and schools, now trying to remain "value-free" (as if that were possible), must not miss the consequential differences and ramifications of communism. Communism is not just another government. It is in no way the moral equal of democracy. It does not even have the same ramifications for atheists as democracy does.

True tolerance must be accurate. It must realize the differences, place relative values on the differences, and not compromise the truth. It can then be correct in its tolerance, tolerating for freedom's sake, not by Pollyannish idiocy.

Tolerance is not only a requirement for righteous citizenship but also the hope of our God of reconciliation. It is what He Himself exercises. Second Peter 3:9 states the reason Christ has not come again: "The Lord is not slow about His promise . . . but is patient toward you, not wishing for any to perish but for all to come to repentance." God now tolerates rebellion and wrong thinking as a provision toward reconciliation. The hope of reconciliation must also be ours. There is no hope, no understanding, no communication without tolerance. Unfortunately, and ironically, many individuals who are the most intense about their faith are the least tolerant. The intensity-intolerance link is a stumbling block to the unbelieving world that looks for the purity of religion and love to be combined. The famous French atheist Voltaire wrote in his *Philosophical Dictionary* (1764), "Of all religions, the Christian is without doubt the one which should inspire tolerance most, although up to now Christians have been the most intolerant of men." This intolerance, reflexively feared by most non-Christians and many other Christians, is simply a product of immaturity.

Most individuals retain an adolescent habit: they define themselves by what they are not. Like middle school children that punctuate their conversations with, "I hate school. . . . He's a jerk. . . . She is so stuck-up. . . . Don't you just hate math?" Christians are much more prone to the negative than the positive. It is easier to state what we do not believe than it is to state what we do believe. It is easier to distance ourselves from who we are not than it is to explain who we are. Hence, identity comes at first from separation. Intolerance is often more a sign of an identity search than a positive stand on any issue. That is true for both individuals and churches.

It is almost axiomatic that the more fervent a local church gets about its faith, or any part of it, the more exclusive it becomes. Intensity is linked to exclusion rather than truth by all who are outside of it because the outsiders are the ones excluded. Yet when most people, nonbelievers included, picture Jesus, they picture Him as loving, gathering, including all.

It is also common that the churches that are most tolerant are the least passionate about what they believe. They prize people, not only above doctrine, but almost to the ignorance of doctrine. They cannot claim spiritual maturity even if they may claim emotional maturity. Yet when most people picture Jesus, they picture Him as not compromising the truth.

In retrospect, the religious crowd of Jesus' day had passion, but insisted on no freedom. That is intolerance. Pilate had no passion; he was nonchalant. That is false tolerance. Jesus spoke the truth and loved without agreement. That is tolerance. The difference between Christians and their Lord is not one of intent, but one of maturity. We have not yet "become conformed to the image of His Son, that He might be the firstborn among many brethren" (Rom. 8:29). When Christians in general can mature to the point that their intensity and inclusiveness combine, they will become agents of true tolerance. They will become a healing presence in politics and everywhere else. There will be a wideness to their worldview while they fix their eyes upon Jesus (Heb. 12:2). There will be a freedom in our ability to understand and a discipline in our thinking. *True tolerance becomes the hallmark of zeal instead of its opposite.* Passion and freedom meet in tolerance, and tolerance sets the stage for reconciliation.

The Pilate Program is a simple procedure for a Christian approaching politics. Procedures, unlike "expert" analyses, give people permission to advance into areas that may be new to them. Procedures keep us from using uncertainty as an excuse for not acting. The assumption in a procedure is that any individual is capable of doing the job, at his own pace. The advantage of this procedure is that it avoids several traditional pitfalls in political participation.

The Pilate Program emphasizes maturity in individual thinking rather than a mindless followership of political experts. Political leaders are and will remain extremely important. We will always hope that people with special abilities and passionate vision can unify the rest of us in common interests and common effort. That is the natural way. Arthur Schlesinger, Jr., writes, "Government throughout human history has always been government by minorities—that is, by elites. This statement is as true for democratic and communistic states today as it was for medieval monarchies and primitive tribes. Masses of people are structurally incapable of directed self-government. They must delegate their power to agents."[4] Leadership is both a need and a desire for most of us. But the best leaders need strong followers, followers who can arrive at political decisions independently. For that, leaders need a procedure. Political decisions are too quickly offered by opinionated commentators and too eagerly sought by the irresolute. Without some think-it-yourself emphasis, followers will be too mindless to prune leadership, and leaders will be too elevated to work for followers.

The Pilate Program emphasizes personal performance of Scripture over public interpretation of Scripture. Christians have confused their responsibility to follow Scripture with their habit of making Scripture the agenda. Thinking is practical, prayer is practical, tolerance is practical, and action is Christlike.

As a procedure, the Pilate Program mitigates our tendency toward all-or-nothing political bulimia. There are times when we are consumed with changing the world, followed by times when we are so stuffed with worldly cares that we want nothing to do with them anymore. A procedure helps us pace our involvement. It emphasizes God's timing, learned in prayer, rather than emergency urgency projected by all heavy political issues.

How can one remember the steps of the Pilate Program until the procedure is well ingrained? Remember that the Pilate Program makes us:

Get away from the confrontational demonstration—to think
Overlook a narrow religious perspective
Observe deep principles rather than shallow politics
Decide in prayer

Act
Tolerate others toward reconciliation

POLITICS.

Notes

1. Robert Booth Fowler, *Religion and Politics in America* (Methuchen, N.J.: Scarecrow, 1984), 48-49.
2. Ibid., 73.
3. Arthur Schlesinger, Jr., *The Cycles of American History* (Boston: Houghton Mifflin, 1986), 21-22.
4. Ibid., 428.

NINE

Proper Expression (and Punctuation) in Politics

One word of truth outweighs the world.

Alexander Solzhenitsyn

She was the strictest teacher I ever had. She wore her hair in a tight bun, and her feet were stuffed in what resembled combat boots. She marched up and down the aisles teaching fear and English composition, in that order. I can remember the value she attached to punctuation.

"The development of your story depends upon the correct separation of thoughts. It must be executed with the appropriate emphasis in expression. Horrible accidents can occur to communication without proper punctuation!" I pictured sentences running headlong into each other because they had no punctuation marks to stop them. Their meanings could barely be seen in the wreckage. Their beautiful little messages, so full of vibrancy and potential, were snuffed out because someone forgot the punctuation. "Even worse," she continued (I held my breath), "can you imagine the misunderstanding that comes with incorrect punctuation?" I pictured a strong proclamation unnerved by a question mark. I pictured a declaration cut to pieces by commas.

OK, so junior high boys may get weird when bored. But proper punctuation, figuratively and literally, will make or break any story. Just so, punctuation will provide the separation and emphasis needed for Christians to express themselves in politics.

My teacher knew that saying the right thing in the wrong place or at the wrong time or in the wrong way can cause problems. So we must be vigilant about the structure of what we say. We need to realize the most constructive expression is one fitly spoken (Proverbs 25:11). It is the expression that is properly emphasized so that it has the maximum effect. If we could ask ourselves what kind of expression is most appropriate for our concern, we would be so much more powerful in our communication. *We need to be concerned with how to express what God has given us.*

Four punctuation marks will serve as an example of how, if living can be aligned with writing, our expression can be sharpened. Think punctuation.

The Shout of the Exclamation Point

Some things need to be shouted! Warnings, surprises, and hurts are causes to lose caution. They are reasons to become, as one politician described himself, a raging moderate. Remember, exclamations are made stronger by contrast. When Jesus shouted, the change from his normal gentle teaching manner was dramatic. This is not so with much political and religious expression. There are some religious leaders and some political leaders who cannot talk without shouting. Their exclamations will go unheeded. People whose every cry is "Wolf!" are ignored eventually, even when there is a wolf. But a raging moderate is a sight to behold and a sound to hear! They realize that for some statements, any punctuation less than exclamation is devaluation.

Warnings need to be shouted! Listen to Jesus preach in Matthew 23. He is speaking out against acts that are culturally acceptable but spiritually empty. He is not teaching in a monotone. He is not simply relaying information in an objective fashion. He is pleading with people to repent, to turn around in their ways. Because of His heartfelt concern for them, He is trying to get them to change. His voice has every indication of intensity, even alarm. He uses the strongest words to provoke their full attention. And Jesus does all of this because He sees clearly the guilt that will be upon them (v. 35). He is trying to tell his nation of the consequences of their actions.

Do you see clearly the consequences of our present pattern of living? If you do, shout it! Detail what you see—causes and effects. Send it to your government representative. Tell it to the church. Say it to your friends. Then leave it to people to decide whether or not they will listen. Maybe the warning is a political one, such as the details of the desolation that will happen to our grandchildren if the national debt continues to increase. Maybe the warning is a moral one, such as the consequences for a society whose main value is pleasure and main goal is retirement. If God has given you a detailed picture of what is happening to us all, warn everyone with written and spoken facts!

Surprises need to be shouted! Blessed are those who are still shocked! The great moments of advancement in our history are those moments when we have been, as a people, appalled. From the abolitionists to the civil rights marchers, from a singular effort such as Jane Addams's Hull House to a national effort such as the response to the Ethiopian famine in the early 1980s, Americans have not failed to respond when they "realized how bad it was." Our capacity for improvement corresponds to our ability to be repulsed or taken aback by what we see. In every Gospel, Jesus is pictured as appalled by the moneychangers in the temple (Matt. 21:12-17; Mark 11:15-18; Luke 19:45-46; John 2:13-22). They had been there for years; so had He. But He still had the capacity to be shocked by profane behavior.

America is losing its ability to be shocked for two reasons. We are being systematically desensitized by the media that pumps out a steady diet of artificial horror and gore. There is so much pictured violence and squalor in television and movie fare that we are becoming used to it. We have read scandal magazines for so long that little surprises us anymore. Additionally, we are becoming so insulated by our prosperity that injustice, moral indifference, and social problems all seem more tacky than emotionally moving. Englishman Alistair Cooke's commentary on *America* records, "I myself think I recognize here several of the symptoms that Edward Gibbon maintained were signs of the decline of Rome and which arose not from external enemies but from inside the country itself. A mounting love of show and luxury. A widening gap between the very rich and the very poor. An obsession with sex . . . exercising military might in places remote from the centers of power . . . the general desire to live off the state. . . . *And, most disturbing of all, a developing moral numbness to vulgarity, violence, and the assault on the simplest human decencies*"[1] (italics mine). Nevertheless, what capacity for shock we still retain should be unleashed with exclamatory emphasis! The emphasis may be required to get a hearing. It will at least let us know we are not entirely callous.

Hurts also need to be shouted! The selective destruction of people should bring a reflexive cry. In the media, the epidemic incidence of drug abuse, the devastation of teenage suicide, the repulsion of the AIDS disease are seen more as items for discussion than hurt. That is a strange, removed reaction. In a world of AIDS, teen suicide, and child pornography, we should hurt with the hurting. How unbecoming that some Christians, whose God loves these people more than they love themselves, are eager to offer a blood-chilling explanation of God's vengeance for sin! Consequences of sin may be unavoidable, but sins are still reason for profound sorrow. Many Christians want to know more than they want to care. *Until we care, it does not matter how much we know.* Unless we proclaim the cause of the hurting, the mission of Christ (Luke 4:18) is still a foreign mission to us.

The effort that many Christians put forth toward protecting

the unborn is to be commended. Whenever the subject of human harm arises, many Christians instinctively assume a defensive stance on abortion. And that is a good thing. We live in a society that is in many ways more sensitive to animal life than human life. Anyone who takes an egg from an eagle's nest is liable to a fine of up to five thousand dollars and a sentence of up to five years in jail. Yet a fertilized human egg is not so protected. The Internal Revenue Service recognizes a cattle breeder's expenses for a calf *from the date of conception*, but our legal system will not give the same protected status to a human baby. We rightly cry out for the protection of the innocent. We rightly shout for others to consider the reverence of even badly deformed life. We rightly shout to protect the disabled from "mercy killing." But let that person be an adult who has participated in his or her own demise, and they are off our route.

Hurt is no less hurt, tragedy is no less tragedy, because it is self-inflicted. It may be more frustrating. It is certainly more complex. But one test of maturity is the ability to be compassionate and steadfast in cases of, as Menninger wrote, *Man Against Himself*. In this nation suicides far outnumber murders every year. Predictably, many of the social problems that the government and the church will be called to resolve will be those of self-destruction. When those who are hurting want help, the church is in a unique position to respond. Government can provide funds and education, but neither funds nor education can root out the problems. The church, stirred by shouts for compassion, can provide funds, education, *and a life-changing experience with Christ*. The exclamation for resolutions, in this case, do not need to be pointed so much at senators as at ministers, elders, church leaders. The church needs to say with her God, "I have surely seen the affliction of My people . . . and have given heed to their cry" (Exod. 3:7).

So there is a place for an exclamation point in the Christian expression. When God speaks in your heart about warning, or surprise, or hurting, speak what He gives you in no uncertain terms. Let your shouts be backed with facts. Then, let them be loud!

The Caution of the Semicolon

The complexity of politics intimidates people. They feel a pressure to have the answer before they think issues through. Most people will either put forth no ideas, or they are pushed to the opposite extreme of needing to appear that they have *the* answer. Like some animals, intimidation leads some of us to blow up to look more fierce than we are and leads others to keep very still, hoping not to be noticed. Both need to be relieved of the pressure of having all the answers before they speak. Both need to realize the value of semicolon statements. These statements only start a thought; then they are continued and refined by another thought.

Semicolon statements are begun with initial statements that immediately stimulate follow-up thoughts. The initiating thoughts are complete, but not entire. The art of making semicolon statements might lead us to our own conclusions about how to use such statements.

Christians often make conclusive political statements; they should instead make *initial* political statements. The former will mandate simple response; the latter will begin development in thinking and maturity. The former gives people the choice to submit or rebel; the latter gives people the opportunity to perfect the statement.

When a local church says, for example, "abortion is wrong," that is a statement that asks for no elaboration. It implies that it is the answer. Of course it is, most evangelicals believe, true. It is a complete truth by itself, but it is not the entire truth. It has an automatic response, but does not engender a full response. It is a period statement. A semicolon statement might be, "For those who believe abortion is wrong there is much work to be done; ________________________________." The sentence expects a continuation. There are several ways to complete it, only one of which has been used by most local churches: "We must prevent it." Deeper thinking provides deeper obligations. M. Scott Peck writes in *The Different Drum*, "There are no simple solutions. Anyone who thinks with integrity on the subject will feel torn apart. On the other hand, there is no question that abortion is murder of a sort and that a policy of abortion on demand does tend to diminish what Albert Schweitzer called 'reverence for life.' On the other hand there is no question as to the magnitude of the suffering that would result for both parents and children if abortion of the misbegotten were not an option. . . . To legally say 'Thou shalt not abort' is simplistic. Something is missing, left out. We cannot with integrity take responsibility away from individuals as to what they will do with their lives and pregnancies and then put it nowhere. The responsibility has to go somewhere. We cannot with integrity say 'Thou shalt not abort' unless we . . . are willing to assume great responsibility for the financial and psychological health of the individual and child to be."[2]

The local church that speaks about abortion needs to leave it unfinished enough that the principals are connected with the principles. The local church that initiates with a truth about any issue deepens the truth with follow-up concerns. The pastor or elders or proper authority in a local church will do well to speak truth for its own improvement. Semicolon statements indicate further development in ideas and people. Semicolon statements indicate that closely related concerns will follow immediately so that what is true can be entire.

A local church serious about initiating statements for political follow-up may want to form a "semicolon committee" (another name might be more stimulating). The task of this committee would be to address issues in such a way that accurate initiating statements could be posed to the congregation. Helpful initiating statements would require factual research, scriptural principles, confirmation from local church authorities, and expectations of follow-up. These initiating statements would be, for many, the confrontations and information required to send many Christians to their prayer closets, thus beginning the Pilate Program. For many local church Christians, a semicolon committee would be the one consistent developer of the political area of their faith; the committee would be the only regular confrontation they hear. The local church can help us all submit one more area of our life to the lordship of Christ; it can if it will.

Another example of a semicolon statement is one between a constituent and his government representative. Many constituents write when they are angry about an issue. The letter sounds like an accusatory exclamation point aimed at intimidating, not informing. That is not the best message to send. But even more constituents do not write at all because they do not have an entire answer. They do not realize that they have the right to express concern without having the complete answer. The most helpful correspondence for a government representative is a semicolon statement. It has the tone of partnership. It expresses what it knows; it does not know it all. It seeks to support in return for support. It seeks to initiate, hoping for fulfillment. Note the differences between these four statements to a public official:

1. If you ignore the threat of smut, you will be responsible for turning our America into a garbage heap!
2. Can't you do anything about pornography?
3. Pornography is such a serious blight on our land that I wish you would do something about it.
4. It would give me great encouragement to think that we could stand together in support of the Commission on Pornography Report; ________________________________.

Which would inspire you most to complete? The above statements are written to illustrate the tone and expectation contained in an expression. Obviously we would not leave a semicolon statement incomplete; the example merely illustrates the openness to partnership. There is a difference between an offering of anger, of ignorance, of opinion, and of partnership. There is a difference between loading all the burden on the congressman (washing your hands of it) and being willing to be connected with him in his efforts for us. There is a consistency of attention implied.

In addition to partnership, semicolon statements imply a steadfastness of thought. Exclamations can be short-lived. Their spokesmen can burn out or get distracted by other issues. People who tend to exclaim can do so in spurts on one subject or, in habit, on every subject. They can be difficult to count on over the long haul. The same can be true of people whose political concerns are mostly questions. If their questions are not addressed within an allotted period of time, they may get discouraged and quit. Those whose political statements are simple declarations may or may not connect them into a coherent and durable pattern of concern. But a semicolon thought, by definition, looks to be followed by another like it. Semicolon communication represents unfaltering, unswerving, purposeful thought. Like the punctuation mark, it will stand out as an irritant until it is completed (see 4 above). Semicolon communication looks to be joined with ideas that develop it to maturity. Semicolon communication is not brainstorming; it is evolving improvement. As such, it is a more welcomed communication, especially in today's society.

Our society is not becoming known for its tenaciousness of thought and effort. Rose Bird, California's former chief justice, has been quoted as saying, "Ours is an amphetamine society, without the stability of an anchor, hurtling from one idea to another, momentarily clinging to them for support, but then discarding them."[3] Paul had the same problem in mind when he admonished Christians, "We are no longer to be children, tossed here and there . . . and carried about by every wind of doctrine" (Eph. 4:14). Indeed, if we could persevere in developing a fraction of our good intentions, any portion of our good ideas, society would see the benefits of steadfastness. People would understand the value of loyalty to an ideal in contrast to the vapor of impulse.

Constituents who communicate a semicolon statement to

their congressman (or pastor or board member or, even, spouse) have a much better chance of response than those who do not. Anyone who considers working with an initiate considers that initiate's stability and resolve. Semicolon statements instill greater confidence for the effort being requested.

One last example of a semicolon statement is intercessory prayer. How can we pray boldly, but not presume to order God? How can we lay our concerns about the government before God, expecting Him to finish and perfect them? Semicolon statements. We need not command God in a shout. That is not prayer; it is arrogance. We need not ask Him questions that require content instead of leading, questions that look for disclosure instead of progress. That is not intercessory prayer; it is curiosity. Neither is intercessory prayer a flat statement to God, informing Him of the world's condition, and, again, washing our hands of the matter. No, when Scripture tells us in 1 Timothy 2:1-2 to make intercession "on behalf of all men, for kings and all who are in authority," it is urging a semicolon stance. That is, it is a positioning of ourselves between the concern we have for the world and what God will do to finish that concern. It yokes our intentions with God's extension. It offers our beginning understanding to His completing response.

Books have been written on the dynamic of intercessory prayer; I speak only to its basic attitude. Whether the prayer be for politics or people, the real intercessor is not just a voice of concern, he is an intermediary looking to be stretched. The goal of the semicolon punctuation mark is to connect and to extend. The goal in religion and politics is to both connect ourselves and extend ourselves.

Semicolon types of communication can be used when the objective is not to stand alone but to team up, and when the objective is not to make the point but to make a start. Some more examples, contrasted with other types of punctuation, may help:

Being a sinner means you'd better turn or burn! *vs.* I asked Christ to make a difference in my life; __________.

What can be done about crime? *vs.* I have a beginning idea that could make a dent in our crime problem; __________.

God, I really think my son is one of your mistakes. *vs.* Lord, I want to stand with You and my son; __________.

There are many different ways those sentences could be completed, but in every case the initiate is involved in the completion. There are times when a prophet stands toe to toe against some legislation, court decision, or sin. In those times it is fitting to declare separation in participation. But many more times our participation calls for us to be linked and stretched by putting forth initiating thoughts.

Semicolons symbolize the best relationship between politics and religion. Church and state are institutions that should not be mixed. But in matters of religion and politics, a semipermeable membrane is more appropriate. That is, politics must not be separated from religious values; religion must not be separated from political responsibility. One matures and completes the other; the connection must be close. Certainly politics and religion cannot be without some separation. They are more distinct, less diluted, with some separation. But close separation is more useful than starting all over when it comes to the other. The semicolon borders are perfect for politicoreligious dialogue.

The Quest of the Question Mark

Questions can be used simply to obtain information, and they should be. But questions have a larger use in political expression. They can be used to provoke thinking and change. Unlike semicolon expression, in which the initiate is linked to the response, questions taken seriously can cause reactions in others regardless of our relationship to them.

Admittedly, many questions used in politics and religion are fake. Much of the time they are, like Pilate's "What is truth?" not really questions at all. They are mere rhetorical points scored in verbal battle. A real question should mark a real search in religion or politics. A probing question can cause a reaction that may be as valuable as the answer. A probing question is a catalyst.

Carl Archdeacon taught me about catalysts; he could teach us all. Anyone traveling through Shelby, Ohio, in the early 1960s could have looked at Mr. Archdeacon and said, "That man is a chemistry teacher." They would have been correct.

Mr. Archdeacon stood behind the counter one afternoon. He was teaching from his usual spot, looking his usual self. His hair was parted down the middle, years after and years before that part was in style His glasses kept creeping down his nose, and he would take his hand off his slide rule just long enough to push them back up. His bow tie divided his faultless mind from his rolled-up white sleeves. And he droned on as I did my usual math research: counting holes in the ceiling tile (I had already counted the blocks in the wall and the pens in his shirt). But this day my math projects would be interrupted. I was stirred, for some reason, by an explanation of a catalyst.

"A catalyst," he said, "is a substance by which a chemical reaction is initiated or accelerated, while the catalyst itself remains unchanged." He went on with examples of an agent that would affect those elements around it but would not itself be changed.

As I began my studies in American history at Ohio University, I noticed that most of the questions asked by the history makers of our country were not information-gathering questions. The questions were more like catalysts, stimulating an action rather than just an answer.

The famous speech of Patrick Henry in 1775 included catalytic questions such as, "Is life so dear or peace so sweet as to be purchased at the price of chains?" That question, followed by his own independent exclamation, "I know not what course others may take, but as for me, give me liberty or give me death!" stirred people to decision and action.

In the Constitutional Convention of 1787, debate continued for over a month without progress, Benjamin Franklin addressed President Washington to ask the delegates catalytic questions: "In this situation of this Assembly, groping as it were in the dark to find political truth, and scarce able to distinguish it when presented to us, how has it happened, Sir, that we have not hitherto once thought of humbly applying to the Father of lights to illuminate our understandings?" After reviewing the historic importance of prayer in our nation's break with Great Britain, he continued, "And have we forgotten that powerful friend? Or do we imagine that we no longer need his assistance? ... God governs in the affairs of men. And if a sparrow cannot fall to the ground without his notice, is it probable that an empire can rise without his aid?" Franklin went on to propose prayer at the beginning of each session. His questions were posed to cause decision and action.

As I grew in Christ, I noticed that many of the questions in Scripture were posed to cause change as much as they were to gather information. God's questions of a sinful man and woman, when examined closely, are catalytic. When God asks, "Where are you?" of man in sin (Gen. 3:9), the question is not one of geography but of biography. The objective is for Adam to change, not for God to increase His store of information. When God asks woman in sin, "What is this you have done?" (v. 13), we must presume He already knows the answer. The objective is to cause her to come to a realization and change. In these cases and others, the information asked for was secondary to the hoped-for reaction. Catalytic questions are real questions, but the answers are not simple. They are deep and moving. Christians can ask great, stirring questions.

Questions can be used in politics and religion in the most profound, influential ways, or toward the most limited, self-serving ends. Questions can cause us to see and act in new ways, or they can be used to manipulate us without our insight. Some questions are not questions at all, but statements in disguise. They are designed to lead us to a predesignated answer, giving us the impression that we reached the conclusion on our own. Really, the answer has no destiny but the question, and the answer depends upon our not thinking.

Such questions are devices. They play upon our emotions, preventing our thinking of anything but the question. They are a sham and a shame. I heard an evangelist once tell about a man who refused to accept Christ and, "that very afternoon his little girl was run over by a car. Do you think that man did not cause his little girl's death?" The question was not asked so that we could explore theological possibilities, or even to examine the character of God. The question was asked to scare people into a yes answer to his coming altar call.

In like manner, politicians will use inflammatory questions to limit thought and exploration. The question "Do we want the communists to take control?" is an almost universal excuse for military action, but it does not stimulate more than one possible answer. Sometimes that question is the bottom line; more often it is the first line. The type of question that limits us to one possible answer while threatening us is not a catalyst; it is a cattle prod.

We have greater possibilities. The questions we ask can generate more than simple answers, sometimes without obtaining any specific answers at all. Serious questions can stimulate change and commitment. Serious questions can summon values and insight. Let us look at some of the questions Jesus asked, to use them as models.

There was a question for believers: "Why are you so timid? How is it that you have no faith?" (Mark 4:40). The question was asked of them when they were afraid of being overwhelmed by threatening forces. It had not occurred to them that they had any power over the situation. But the question posed by Jesus was never answered directly. Instead, it was a catalyst for a deeper question: "Who then is this, that even the wind and sea obey Him?" (v. 41). Evidently, the more they looked inside themselves, the more they wanted to know about Christ's power.

The question is appropriate today, especially in the church. Why are we so timid? How is it that we have no faith? Questions like that are needed to reveal our sense of powerlessness and fear. If we listen to the news daily and read the headlines, we may feel overwhelmed. We may feel powerless to make any difference at all. But the question is not one of power, it is one of faith. The real investigation is not so much into human potential as it is into who God is in this situation. And why aren't we directly calling on Him, for either guidance or divine intervention or insight? The *why* from questions like that hardly ever result in a specific answer. Yet it is a catalyst that will activate us into a new boldness with God and His power in the world.

There was a question for the culture: "Why does this generation seek for a sign?" (Mark 8:12). The request for some show of what Jesus could do for them was made by the Pharisees, but it represented the entire generation. It is not an irrelevant question to our culture so fixated on the superficial. Its answer is legion; there is no simple direct answer. The question, though, is a summary of the culture's mentality. It is a catalyst to make us question our showy, but vacant, values.

In our quest for the physical (usually monetary) things, our culture needs to have questions posed like, "Why do we seek mainly for physical, visible differences? Is that all we can comprehend? What are the spiritual opportunities now available that will make a more profound difference in our life than anything physical? What do the signs we seek represent? Then what is really important?" Such questions are an antidote to shallowness.

Some questions can be answered, but not left at the answer. The answer is a command for further action. It is a catalyst that prompts change all around it, while remaining separated (holy) from change itself. The answer is more influential than informational. Thus, the question is a most valuable one.

Questions, then, are so very useful in punctuating religiopolitical expression. The catalyst type of question, even more than the facts type of question, serves to stimulate change. We need to ask questions to Christians in world chaos (politics) to make sure they are being bold in God's strength. We need to ask questions of the generation looking to visibly change the world through politics, to probe for values underneath goals. And we need to ask questions that will call for a summary of different understandings but a firm stand in the midst of them.

None of these questions are neutralized by one-time answers. They are always relevant, always causing deep reactions. They prevent a mindless, run-on faith, making us stop and think. It is our job to ask them, listening for an answer and, even more, planting an influence. Who else will do it?

The Need for Response

All three types of political expression that have just been discussed look for a response. An exclamation point attracts attention to emergency issues. A semicolon looks for some sort of development of the thought it has initiated. A catalytic question hopes for a reaction, as much as an answer, that will change the inner chemistry of our political solutions. Thus all of these expressions have a character of incompleteness. They have the typical tentativeness of political struggle and religious request. Their objectives can be denied. They are risks. They do reflect righteous efforts to change the world, but they may well get no immediate response. So political expression by Christians may appear to be at the mercy of cultural receptivity, and, in one sense, it is. The response to any of these types of expression can be withheld, or negative. The effort put into them and the emotional investment, may appear to be wasted. That is why Christian political expression over the years has been a sporadic participant in American history. Christians require a certain amount of success, or at least response, for their efforts, or they get discouraged and confine their religious expressions to church. That is also why political expression must be a matter of obedience instead of courage or hope. Obedience is consistent no matter what the response; courage and hope sometimes flag when the winds of response stop. So it is that these expressions toward attention, development, or reaction may appear to fail in one sense and leave their authors discouraged. There is, however, one more type of political expression that is not so dependent.

Many of us look for strong, orthodox rules of thumb in the political realm. We all desire some statements that do not need to be corrected or retracted. We all would respect some truths that cannot be swept aside or ignored. Short-term political answers, no matter how strong, do not fit into this category. Instead, statements of historical perspective and truth can provide the strong leadership compass we all need. Think long.

Statements are expressions that need no response. By statements I mean foundational truths that summarize what our Author has said in His Word. Statements do not need to use Scripture to endorse a greater point; statements are the truths woven throughout Scripture. They are truths "we hold to be self-evident." Statements need no hype, for they are themselves a source of encouragement. Statements remind us of God's fundamental structure of the world, so that our attempts at political solutions have both proper perspective and utilitarian value. Two seem especially relevant here: individual maturity and the sovereignty of God.

Individual Maturity Is Key

We need to declare the tremendous importance of individual maturity in Christian political involvement. Scripture and experience are witness to one conclusion: there is neither a political solution nor a political system that is adequate in all circumstances and times. Rather, the key is the mature individual, or group of them, that can fit a solution or system to the common good. What to think is not as valuable as how to think.

Christianity has a unique view of the importance of individuality. Christianity differs from Eastern religions in the attention given to individuality. The goal in Eastern religions is to escape this world and eliminate the self. The goal of Christianity is to take care of this world and purify the self for the eternal dwelling with God. Christianity is also distinct from Judaism in the amount of attention given to the individual's development as differentiated from the development of a holy nation. The holy nation concern is still present in the New Testament, but there is less of a herd instinct insinuated. Instead, the holy nation is formed by individual commitment (Luke 3:8) and individual obedience empowered by the endowment of the individual with the Holy Spirit (Acts 2:38). The unity comes from the Spirit (Eph. 4:3) instead of human agreement about goals, or political systems that unite "under God." So the holy nation is a result of individual holiness and not the cause of it. And the responsibility given to the individual cannot be taken away by the group without crippling the group.

In many ways, the democracy of the United States reflects many of the same concerns as Christianity. Its attention to the rights of individuals, and its dependence upon the input of individuals, implies its understanding of the centrality of the individual. That has been both its strength and its weakness, for the American system is devised to accommodate individuals, not to mature them. So it is that the immaturity of Americans who expect a great government without building one may render our democracy impotent.

Group policy may be a reflection of the maturity of the individuals who composed it, but it can never be a replacement for the maturity of the individuals who live under it. The bane of our country and our Christianity is that we respect the wisdom of the Founding Father(s) so much that we desire to idolize it instead of emulate it. Which of our Founding Fathers did not pay his "pound of flesh" to improve this country, and, having rid himself of that much flesh, was not enlarged in spirit? Which of the apostles, in struggling with group issues (see Acts 10 and 11), did not mature by wrestling with group policy? Somehow, we must communicate that the group arena is a training ground for individual responsibility and maturity. The goal is not the "right policy," set by a Herculean effort followed by a Rip van Winkle rest. The goal is to allow the individual to consistently address group needs as well as his own and to mature in this earthly journey because of it. Let us observe the following balance.

Christians in politics need to know the importance of promoting individual maturity above group fixes. We need to acknowledge that public policy has only secondhand impact upon the lives of individuals. It does not give inner direction on how to live; it is a boundary in which to live. The ideal of "Christian public policy," where it has existed, has been a placebo. It does make some difference, especially from a psychological point of view. But it is more a comfort than an actual aid. It looks like good medicine, but, in the long run, its main power is in its ability to encourage rather than to cure. And its main danger is that it may take the place of real medicine. The "right policy" can become a pernicious substitute, in that it is seen as a replacement for the real cure—Jesus Christ in an individual's life. Thus, if we would do people the most good, we cannot depend on group policy.

No matter what the public policies are, the Christian's work will not be changed. There is no real improvement in society without individual spiritual development, and our work is to individuals. If some government decision happens to be "pro-Christian," it could make our work a little easier. If, instead, it is "anti-Christian," it could make our work a little more difficult. But the content of our work remains the same. No government decision, even the Supreme Court's decision for abortion, can replace the need for attention to an individual's life and growth. So the individual, not the group, is always the primary preoccupation of our efforts. Those efforts, if mature, are not radically affected by public policy.

The other side of that balance is that individual maturity is also key in our building of group policy. Having recognized the primacy of individual care from individuals, we must also recognize the importance of individual responsibility toward the government. The government may have only a secondhand impact on our lives, but that is still a significant impact.

We care about its policies for two very important reasons: because we care about individuals as a whole (James 2:15-16) and because God has given each of us a responsibility in taking care of his world (Mark 13:34).

What part of a person's life is the spiritual part? I cannot find any dividing line in a human life. Every influence upon an individual chisels one more mark on his character. Maturity comprehends the complex interaction of the various influences and cares about them all. Maturity does what it can toward the person's environment, as well as toward the person himself, as an act of love. That includes addressing government policy. Such group focus must always be the minor and not the major of our efforts, unless we have been called to a ministry of public service. But, in all cases, government is important for the sake of individuals and our ministry toward them.

Also, stewardship of this world is not a choice, it is an order. God does not give us all the same responsibilities, but part of our maturing is the addressing of His direct orders, in teamwork, for the care of his world until He returns. "It is like a man, away on a journey, who upon leaving his house and putting his slaves in charge, assigning to each one his task, also commanded the doorkeeper to stay on the alert" (Mark 13:34). Maturity knows this is not my nation, not my world, just my responsibility. And maturity knows He's coming back.

The development of individual maturity cannot come in fantasies of group fixes nor in limitations to "spiritual work" only. The development of individual maturity comes in inclusive thinking and intense effort for individuals, in the public arena as well as the private relationship. When we address politics, individual maturity is both the requirement and the goal.

God Is Sovereign

Christianity also has a unique view of history. God in Christ stands at the end of every individual's earthly life. God in Christ also stands at the end of history in general. No matter what one's particular eschatology may be, not many Christians would dispute these two facts disclosed in Scripture. It is because of these two facts, woven throughout Scripture, that we can assume that the end is woven throughout the present. God, says Scripture, is one who designed history for a purpose and is active in history. The participation of God in history is clear from the Incarnation (John 1:14). The development of history is clear from such concepts as His acting in the ripeness of time (Gal. 4:4). Therefore, we are not orphans, and the events of this world are not removed from the God "who works all things after the counsel of His will" (Eph. 1:11).

We can clearly state to the world that God is in control. That may likely confuse many, but it puts the correct perspective on history. The Eastern religions' cyclical view of history, one in which all hope to cycle into nothingness, is antithetical to the Judeo-Christian view. Our firm faith, made upon the authority of Scripture, is that God uses the events of this world to develop individuals and history toward His purposes. When we understand that, politics acquires a different meaning. He uses our efforts, no matter how minimal they seem.

Politics, for Christians, is meant to be a test instead of a temptation. A test is a vehicle used for perfecting us and, hopefully, God's world (James 1:2-4). Tests are difficult, by nature, yet extremely useful in showing us both what we have and have not mastered. Our reactions to the world will manifest Christ to the extent we obey Him and to the extent we expect Him to come in history. Peter writes in a letter whose context is political persecution, "Beloved, do not be surprised at the fiery ordeal among you, which comes upon you for your testing, as though some strange thing were happening to you; but to the degree that you share the sufferings of Christ, keep on rejoicing; so that also at the revelation of His glory, you may rejoice with exultation" (1 Pet. 4:12-13). Our temptation is to ignore political progress or to cling to it. Our test is to share Christ's ministry in politics, realizing that the resultant policy is not outside God's historical plan.

"Then," you say, "the outcome of the world doesn't really matter. It is just individual perfection that we are after." No, God is working in all of history to bring it to Himself (2 Pet. 3:9). He is able in time to bring victory out of defeat, and He will in history be victorious. We must tell that to any who will hear.

Sometimes that is rather difficult to believe. Political power looks so attractive and those who have it look so strong. Christians tend to feel deflated when they are defeated. But the God who used the cross for victory can use any weakness for power. A man once told me to take a serious look at history for a simple illustration of God's sovereign power.

"If I could take you back in time," he said, "to Rome, about A.D. 60, you might stand in a street and see two buildings. One would be a prison; inside would be a dark, damp cell holding one little man with a physical deformity. His name: Paul. He would be writing his testamentary letters to the church at Philippi and to his friend Philemon. When his eyes got tired, he might try to tell the prison guard about this Jesus, the Christ, who had changed his life. Rebuffed, he might sit to write again, knowing he would not give up on that guard.

"If you would look across the street, you would see the most glorious sight—the Coliseum. It would be filled with hundreds and hundreds of Rome's best citizens, all waiting for one man to enter. That man would be the ruler of the most powerful empire the world had ever seen. When that one man entered, all would stand to salute in a thunderous roar, 'Hail Caesar! Hail Caesar!'

"If you were asked to choose the more powerful man then, to which side of the street would you turn? Yet, thousands of years later, people are naming their children Paul and their dogs Caesar."

Above all the work we have yet to do, underneath all the expressions toward political progress we have yet to make, we need to know that individual maturity and God's sovereignty are, in the end, unbeatable. Period.

Notes

1. Alistair Cooke, *Alistair Cooke's America* (New York: Knopf, 1973), 387.
2. M. Scott Peck, *The Different Drum: Community Making and Peace* (New York: Simon and Schuster, 1987), 247.
3. U.S. *News & World Report*, 13 July 1987, 13.

TEN

"In Deed": A Workbook for Political Involvement

The future is purchased by the present.

Samuel Johnson

Americans have, from the beginning, been concerned about the practicality of thought. American Christians have, from the beginning, been concerned about the practicality of theology. Historian Daniel Boorstin writes of the Puritans, "Their orthodoxy had a peculiar character ... what really distinguished them in their day was that they were less interested in theology itself, than in the application of theology to everyday life, and especially to society. From the seventeenth-century point of view their interest in theology was practical. They were less concerned with perfecting their formulation of the Truth than with making their society in America embody the Truth they already knew. Puritan New England was a noble experiment in applied theology."[1]

This book concludes within that heritage. The American experience has been one of the freedom of experiment. Christianity has a history of being a strong voice in that experiment, and we hope the voice will become even stronger. As long as we do not try to exchange the Holy Spirit for the government as the means of conversion, God will use Christians for depth and improvement in our civil government. That is, He will if we are willing.

For those who are ready to use the Pilate Program outlined in chapters 7 and 8 and who desire to sharpen their punctuation skills as outlined in chapter 9, I offer the following pages. Herein, a Christian will find practical information to use in becoming competent in politics.

Basic References: My Government Organization

The following reference list can be completed, for the most part, by looking in your phone book in the "Governmental Offices" section.

I. *Voter Registration* ______________________

(Phone to inquire where to register. Also ask if the registration is permanent or needs to be renewed. When one registers, information about where to vote, in what district one is a resident, who one's representatives are, etc. may also be obtained.)

II. *Neighborhood/Homeowners/Condominium Organizations, etc.*

A. Name of Officer ______________________

____
ADDRESS PHONE

B. Usual Concerns Addressed: Neighborhood dues and uses of dues, neighborhood policies, input for improvement, etc.

III. *School Board*

A. County Office ______________________

B. School Board (obtained by calling county office)

1. ______________________
NAME PHONE

2. ______________________
NAME PHONE

3. ______________________
NAME PHONE

4. ______________________
NAME PHONE

5. ______________________
NAME PHONE

6. ____
NAME PHONE
7. ____
NAME PHONE

C. Usual Concerns Addressed: Matters concerning local school curriculum, buildings, personnel, policies.

D. PTA President

____
NAME PHONE

IV. *City/Town Government*

A. Important Department Phone Numbers

1. Police ______________ Emergency ______________

2. Fire ______________ Emergency ______________

3. Administrative ______________________________

4. Public Works (streets, sanitation, etc.) ____________

5. Development (building, zoning, planning) ________

6. Miscellaneous ______________________________

B. Officials

1. Mayor/Manager

____
NAME PHONE

2. Commissioners

____
NAME PHONE

3. Clerk

____
NAME PHONE

4. Miscellaneous

____

C. Usual Concerns Addressed: Services such as police, fire, parks, libraries, streets, water, garbage, health protection, business regulation, zoning, etc.

V. *County Government*

A. Important Department Phone Numbers

1. Courthouse ______

2. County Services ______

3. Tag Offices ______

4. County Commission ______

5. County Attorney ______

6. Fire ______

7. Sheriff ______

8. Miscellaneous ______

B. Officials—Commissioners/Managers

NAME PHONE

NAME PHONE

NAME PHONE

NAME PHONE

NAME PHONE

NAME PHONE

C. Usual Concerns Addressed: County responsibilities such as education, parks, welfare, hospitals, health care, zoning, taxes, records, fire, police, environment, licenses, etc.

VI. *State Government*

A. Important Department Phone Numbers

1. Governor's Office ______

2. Miscellaneous ______

______

B. Important Officials

1. Governor ____________________

____
ADDRESS PHONE

2. State Legislators

a. Representative ____________________

____
ADDRESS PHONE

b. Senator ____________________

____
ADDRESS PHONE

C. Usual Concerns Addressed: Education laws (major responsibility), public utilities regulation, highways, police and jails, welfare, health and hospital concerns, environment, business regulations, taxes, etc.

VII. *Federal Government*

A. Important Department Numbers (toll free)

1. Internal Revenue Service ____________________

2. Problem Resolution Office ____________________

3. Miscellaneous ____________________

____

B. Legislators

1. Representative ____________________

____
WASHINGTON OFFICE ADDRESS PHONE

____
LOCAL OFFICE ADDRESS PHONE

2. Senator ____________________

____
WASHINGTON OFFICE ADDRESS PHONE

____
LOCAL OFFICE ADDRESS PHONE

3. Senator ____________________

____
WASHINGTON OFFICE ADDRESS PHONE

____
LOCAL OFFICE ADDRESS PHONE

C. President
The White House
1600 Pennsylvania Avenue
Washington, DC 20500
Phone (202) 456-1414

D. Usual Concerns Addressed: Matters dealing with federal policy, such as taxes, foreign policy, federal law, human services, etc.

VIII. *Church–Political Concerns*

A. Church Office Phone ____________________

B. Officials

1. Pastor ____________________

____
ADDRESS PHONE

2. "Political Concerns" Leader

____
ADDRESS PHONE

3. "Semicolon Committee" Members:

a. Name ____________________

____
ADDRESS PHONE

b. Name ____________________

____
ADDRESS PHONE

c. Name ____________________

____
ADDRESS PHONE

d. Name ______________________________

____
ADDRESS PHONE

e. Name ______________________________

____
ADDRESS PHONE

f. Name ______________________________

____
ADDRESS PHONE

C. Usual Concerns Addressed: Matters concerning our stewardship of God's world in His way, especially those of a direct Christian-political nature.

IX. *Specific Concerns Group* (*advocacy or interest groups*)

A. Group ______________________________

____
ADDRESS PHONE

B. Group ______________________________

____
ADDRESS PHONE

C. Group ______________________________

____
ADDRESS PHONE

D. Group ______________________________

____
ADDRESS PHONE

X. *Media References*

A. Newspapers

1. Name ______________________________

____
LETTERS TO THE EDITOR ADDRESS

____
PHONE

2. Name ____________________

____
LETTERS TO THE EDITOR ADDRESS

____
PHONE

3. Name ____________________

____
LETTERS TO THE EDITOR ADDRESS

____
PHONE

B. Radio Stations

1. Station ____________________

____
ADDRESS PHONE

Program Manager ____________________

____
ADDRESS PHONE

2. Station ____________________

____
ADDRESS PHONE

Program Manager ____________________

____
ADDRESS PHONE

3. Station ____________________

____
ADDRESS PHONE

Program Manager ____________________

____
ADDRESS PHONE

C. Television Stations

1. Station ____________________

____
ADDRESS PHONE

General Manager ____________________

____
PHONE

Program Manager ____________________

____
PHONE

News Coordinator ____________________

____
PHONE

2. Station ____________________

____
ADDRESS PHONE

General Manager ____________________

____
PHONE

Program Manager ____________________

____
PHONE

News Coordinator ____________________

____
PHONE

3. Station ____________________

____
ADDRESS PHONE

Program Manager ____________________

____
PHONE

Program Manager ____________________

____
PHONE

News Coordinator ____________________

____
PHONE

Basic Resources: My Information Infusion

Being informed about political issues is relatively free and simple, but it requires regular discipline. Our local library is the center of all the information we need; our local church can be the center for Christian political discussion.

I. *The Library Connection*

A. The Newspapers: Print information is valuable for deeper consideration of political information than television usually allows. Major metropolitan newspapers offer up-to-date information about specific issues that God may be bringing to your attention for prayer. Most libraries carry such major newspapers as the *New York Times* and others. *The Christian Science Monitor* is a widely respected national newspaper. Many larger libraries also receive copies of newspapers from Europe and Canada.

B. The Periodicals: Your library will have a list of the periodicals they receive in both the political science area and in the religion area. A spectrum of the more commonly accepted resources enabling Christian-political involvement include:

1. Secular:
   a. U.S. *News & World Report*; *Time*; *Newsweek*
   b. *The National Review*; *The New American* (conservative)
   c. *The New Republic* (liberal)
   d. *World Press Review*
2. Christian:
   a. *Christianity Today* (evangelical)
   b. *The Christian Century* (liberal)
   c. *Sojourners*
   d. *Commonweal*
   e. *Eternity* (evangelical)

C. *The Congressional Quarterly Weekly*: Your library no doubt subscribes to this crucial publication. It arrives weekly and has as close to an unbiased perspective as possible. It examines important issues, informs of upcoming issues (so we may know in advance to write our congressmen), and it reports how our congressmen voted on the issues. It is too expensive for most Americans to subscribe to (just under $1,000 annually), but it is free at the library.

Also, the library has a volume published from the *Congressional Quarterly* called *Politics in America*. This volume contains biographical information about congressmen and how they are rated by various groups.

D. Various books in the field of Christians in politics (see Bibliography).

E. A resource librarian to help you find, specifically, the information you need.

II. *The Home Connection*

A. Television News and Specials: Though television journalism is thought to have anti-Christian bias in the name of being unbiased, it serves us all in several ways:

1. Certain cable stations, such as C-SPAN, give uncommentaried, live coverage of Congress and other government action. This is the best source of information on TV.
2. TV has the most up-to-date information available.
3. TV does tend to "confront" us personally with graphic portrayals of issues; hence it engenders involvement.
4. TV makes us familiar with the most culturally popular issues and mind-set so that we can be realistic in our political approach.
5. Programs like William F. Buckley's "Firing Line" (PBS) provide opportunities to hear public figures speak for themselves with some depth.

B. Newspapers and Periodicals: Both are affordable to many families and can engender discussion within the family. Spiritual and civic concerns can be taught from an in-family discussion of the facts.

C. Radio Programs: Certain radio programs, from "All Things Considered" on public radio stations to the most conservative Christian call-in programs, are available to raise our awareness.

D. Discussions: Trading news and opinions with relatives, neighbors, and friends is still a potent means of being informed.

III. *The Church Connection*

A. Check to see if your church has any forum for Christian-political dialogue. Perhaps God is calling you to pray about that kind of addition.

B. Your church may have some sort of "semicolon committee" charged with bringing political issues to the congregation. If so, what can we learn from them? What kind of follow-up is needed?

C. Your political leaning should look to a spiritual authority for its development. God gives us directions; spiritually mature counselors help us in our implementation of them. You may desire to develop an idea or get biblical counsel about your concerns. Talk to your pastor or designated "elder" in the Lord.

D. A trusted Bible teacher (if you don't have one, the church can direct you to one) will help connect relevant biblical passages to your political concern. One of the basic questions of every Christian when it comes to any issue needs to be, What does the Bible say about this? though sometimes the answer will be, Nothing directly.

Basic Questions: My Primary Concerns

Since some people would say that every issue and every candidate has direct religious implications, and other people would say only a very few issues or candidates have any direct religious impact, a few questions will clarify *your* calling.

I. *On Issues*

A. Where can this issue be found repeatedly in Scripture?

B. What affect will this issue have on the Christian cause?

C. How much impact would a solution to this issue have on the lives of people? Who will it benefit? Who will it hurt?
D. How much of my time should be spent on it?

II. *On Candidates*
A. What religious impact does this person have?
B. How does his/her voting record match my Christian values?
C. What is his/her personal example?
D. What interests do his/her supporters have?
E. What is God calling me to do for this candidate?

III. *On Self*
A. What are my motives when I address this issue/candidate?
B. Am I afraid of something? Why?
C. Am I trying to control something? To what end?
D. From whom am I getting my opinion?
E. Who is the object of my action? Me? A group? God?
F. What can I learn from—and do for—the other side?

Basic Directions: The Lord in My Life

Keeping a record of the Spirit's leadings toward the political arena is a way of keeping ourselves accountable for follow-through. Here is one idea for such a diary.

I. *Impressions from daily quiet time for political participation*

A. ____

B. ____

C. ____

II. *Burdens from being confronted—pray for direction*

A. ____

B. ____

C. ____

III. *God's leading for action and what type of punctuation—! or ; or ?*

A. ______________________________

B. ______________________________

C. ______________________________

IV. *Actions taken*

A. ______________________________

Results ______________________________

B. ______________________________

Results ______________________________

C. ______________________________

Results ______________________________

V. *Acts of Reconciliation/Tolerance*

A. The other side is ______________________________

B. The other side is ______________________________

C. The other side is ______________________________

VI. *Accountability*
Knowing I may need encouragement or help in participating politically, I will ask ______________ to hold me accountable for this area of my Christian development.

Bibliography

Alley, Robert S. *So Help Me God*. Richmond: John Knox, 1972.

Boorstin, Daniel J. *The Colonial Experience*. New York: Vintage, 1964.

———. *The Image: A Guide to Pseudo-Events in America*. New York: Harper, 1961.

Brentano, Frances. *Nation Under God*. Great Neck, N.Y.: Channel Press, 1957.

Brown, Robert McAfee. *Saying Yes and Saying No*. Philadelphia: Westminster, 1986.

Buttrick, George Arthur, ed. *The Interpreter's Dictionary of the Bible*. Nashville: Abingdon, 1962.

Carpenter, Edmund, and Ken Heyman. *They Became What They Beheld*. New York: Ballantine, 1970.

Colson, Charles. *Kingdoms in Conflict*. Grand Rapids and New York: Zondervan and Morrow, 1987.

Cooke, Alistair. *Alistair Cooke's America*. New York: Knopf, 1973.

Cotham, Perry C. *Politics, Americanism, and Christianity*. Grand Rapids: Baker, 1976.

Cousins, Norman. *In God We Trust: The Religious Beliefs and Ideas of the American Founding Fathers*. New York: Harper, 1958.

Dahl, Robert. *Who Governs? Democracy and Power in an American City*. New Haven: Yale University Press, 1961.

Duke, Paul, ed. *Beyond Reagan: The Politics of Upheaval*. New York: Warner Books, 1986.

Falwell, Jerry. *Listen, America!* New York: Bantam, 1980.

Garraty, John A. *The American Nation: A History of the United States.* New York: Harper, 1966.

Hatfield, Mark. *Between a Rock and a Hard Place.* Waco, Tex.: Word, 1976.

Hill, Samuel S., and Dennis E. Owen. *The New Religious-Political Right in America.* Nashville: Abingdon, 1982.

Hofstadter, Richard. *The American Political Tradition.* New York: Vintage, 1948.

Hutchins, Robert M., ed. *Great Books of the Western World.* Chicago: Encyclopedia Britannica, 1952.

Kater, John. *Christians on the Right: The Moral Majority in Perspective.* New York: Seabury, 1982.

Kegley, Charles W., and Robert W. Bretall, eds. *Reinhold Niebuhr: His Religious, Social, and Political Thought.* New York: Macmillan, 1956.

Kronenwetter, Michael. *Politics and the Press.* New York: Franklin Watts, 1987.

LaHaye, Tim. *The Hidden Censors.* Old Tappan, N.J.: Revell, 1984.

Lasch, Christopher. *The Culture of Narcissism.* New York: Warner Books, 1979.

Latourette, Kenneth Scott. *A History of Christianity.* 1953. Reprint in 2 vols. New York: Harper and Row, 1975.

Lichter, S. Robert, Stanley Rothman, and Linda S. Lichter. *The Media Elite: America's New Pawnbrokers.* Bethesda, Md.: Adler and Adler, 1986.

Loeb, Marshall, and William Safire. *Plunging into Politics: How to Become or Support a Candidate on the National, State, or Local Level.* New York: David McKay, 1964.

Love, Thomas T., and John Courtney Murray. *Contemporary Church-State Theory.* Garden City, N.Y.: Doubleday, 1965.

Marshall, Peter, and David Manuel. *The Light and the Glory.* Old Tappan, N.J.: Revell, 1977.

Menninger, Karl. *Whatever Became of Sin?* New York: Hawthorn, 1973.

———. *Man Against Himself.* New York: Harcourt, Brace and World, 1966.

Merriam, Robert C., and Rachel M. Goetz. *Going into Politics: A Guide for Citizens*. New York: Harper, 1957.

Milbrath, Lester W., and M. I. Goel. *Political Participation: How and Why Do People Get Involved in Politics?* Chicago: Rand McNally, 1977.

Muehl, William. *Politics for Christians*. New York: Haddam House Association, 1956.

Muggeridge, Malcolm. *Christ and the Media*. Grand Rapids: Eerdmans, 1977.

Mulcahy, Kevin V., and Richard S. Katz. *America Votes: What You Should Know About Elections Today*. Englewood Cliffs, N.J.: Prentice-Hall, 1976.

Neuhaus, Richard John. *The Naked Public Square: Religion and Democracy in America*. Grand Rapids: Eerdmans, 1984.

Niebuhr, H. Richard. *Christ and Culture*. New York: Harper, 1951.

Niebuhr, Reinhold. *Christian Realism and Political Problems*. New York: Scribner's, 1953.

Noll, Mark A. *One Nation under God? Christian Faith and Political Action in America*. San Francisco: Harper and Row, 1988.

Peck, M. Scott. *The Different Drum: Community Making and Peace*. New York: Simon and Schuster, 1987.

———. *People of the Lie*. New York: Simon and Schuster, 1983.

———. *The Road Less Traveled*. New York: Simon and Schuster, 1978.

Peter, Laurence J. *The Peter Pyramid*. New York: William Morrow, 1986.

Pierard, Richard V., Robert G. Clouse, and Robert D. Linder. *The Cross and the Flag*. Carol Stream, Ill.: Creation House, 1972.

Rauschenbusch, Walter. *A Theology for the Social Gospel*. New York: Macmillan, 1917.

Robertson, Pat. *America's Dates with Destiny*. Nashville: Thomas Nelson, 1986.

Schaeffer, Franky. *A Time for Anger: The Myth of Neutrality*. Westchester, Ill.: Crossway, 1982.

Schlesinger, Arthur M., Jr. *The Cycles of American History*. Boston: Houghton Mifflin, 1986.

Schwartz, Tony. *The Responsive Chord*. Garden City, N.Y.: Doubleday, 1974.

Sherwin, Oscar. *Prophet of Liberty: The Life and Times of Wendell Phillips*. New York: Bookman Associates, 1958.

Sorokin, Pitirim A., and Walter A. Lunden. *Power and Morality: Who Shall Guard the Guardians?* Boston: Porter Sargent, 1959.

Sperry, Willard L. *Religion in America*. New York: Macmillan, 1946.

Stanmeyer, William A. *Clear and Present Danger: Church and State in Post-Christian America*. Ann Arbor: Servant Books, 1983.

Stewart, Elbert W., and James A. Glynn. *Introduction to Sociology*. New York: McGraw-Hill, 1985.

Tierney, Brian. *The Crisis of Church and State* 1050–1300. Englewood Cliffs, N.J.: Prentice-Hall, 1964.

Toynbee, Arnold. *An Historian's Approach to Religion*. London: Oxford University Press, 1956.

Udvari, Stephen S. *Being an Informed Citizen*. Austin, Tex.: Steck-Vaughn, 1978.

Vaillancourt, Beverly. *Government Today*. Syracuse: New Readers Press, 1985.

Webber, Robert E. *The Church in the World*. Grand Rapids: Zondervan, 1986.

——— *The Secular Saint: The Role of the Christian in the Secular World*. Grand Rapids: Zondervan, 1979.

A Closing Thought

We live in a world of transgressions and selfishness, and no pictures that represent us otherwise can be true; though happily for human nature, gleamings of that pure spirit, in whose likeness man has been fashioned, are to be seen, relieving its deformities, and mitigating, if not excusing, its crimes.

James Fenimore Cooper